WEARABLE
Wonders

WEAR

ABLE
onders

by Fifi Colston

For my mum, who kept me supplied with paints, glue and tape and taught me how to sew, and my Aunty Isobel, who showed me how to find the glorious potential in a bag full of felt and feathers.
I owe you wonderful women both so much XXX

Useful Links

World of WearableArt: **www.worldofwearableart.com**

Weta Workshop: **www.wetanz.com**

Flax weaving: **www.alibrown.nz**

www.fificreative.com
facebook.com/creativefifi

First published in 2013 by Scholastic New Zealand Limited
Private Bag 94407, Botany, Auckland 2163, New Zealand

This edition published 2025 by Silver Thimble Press
Wellington New Zealand

Text & illustrations © Fifi Colston, 2013

ISBN 978-0-473-72185-5

We acknowledge the following trademarks used in the book: Lycra™ (Invista), Dacron® (DuPont), Velcro® (Velcro Industries BV).

Illustrations created by hand and Adobe Illustrator

Designer: Vida & Luke Kelly
Typeset in ITC Stone Informal, 11/15pt

Wow yourself every day!
xx Fifi.C

Credits: p49 Felt hats by Jean Burgers, Wellington; p54 'Hooking Up' by Penny Linton (age 12); p65 'Tell Tail Tit' by Alice Linton (age 14); p76 Beth Jones, Upper Hutt (model); p78 'Kunugi Kodama' (Photo: World of WearableArt Ltd); p79 'Is it Socks' by Alison Mackay & Gabrielle Edmonds, Lower Hutt, Backstage World of Wearable Arts Award Show (Photos: World of WearableArt Ltd); p82 'I Feel Like a Princess Tonight' by Swati Gupta, India (Photo: World of WearableArt Ltd). All other photographs and illustrations in this book © Fifi Colston.

CONTENTS

WHERE IT ALL BEGAN

When I was six years old, I went to a fancy dress party. All the kids were dressed as fairies and cowboys and I was no exception. I wore my very best pale blue party dress and my mother made me a tinsel wand. I can't remember if I had wings but I do recall being very disappointed with my outfit from the minute I arrived. All the girls had tutus and sparkly crowns. I don't know where their mums managed to find them as we were living in West Africa at the time and there weren't any places to buy costumes there.

But from that moment I decided that if I was going to dress up, I would do it better and more creatively than anyone else. I was a determined child!

There wasn't always money to spend on fancy material and clever trims, so I made do with anything I could find. I was a hoarder of bits and bobs and things that might come in useful one day. If you opened my wardrobe door, bags of feathers scavenged from the local chicken farm, fabric scraps and buttons from old clothes, cereal boxes and plastic yoghurt cartons would all tumble out.

I spent all my spare time making things and learned what would stay together with glue, what would need stitching and what kind of paints would work on different materials.

I've made fancy dress and costume for all of my life since: for film, television, theatre and most often just for fun. Since discovering the World of WearableArt™ in 1995, I have found great joy in creating garments for the yearly show.

With this book, I'm not going to show you how to copy one of my masterpieces. There are no patterns for fairies, cowboys, dragons or sea creatures. Instead, I'm going to show you how you can come up with an idea for something you'd never dreamed of making before, and the way to make a Wearable Wonder of your own.

'Kunugi Kodama' by Fifi Colston.

A GOOD IDEA!

How do I find one and where do I look?

um...

Coming up with an idea is really hard when you have a blank piece of paper in front of you. So right now, forget the sketch book and look around you.

Search the world you know

What can you see? A toy on the floor? A sleeping cat? A chocolate wrapper, or perhaps a pencil with the end half chewed?

These are everyday things that can have a whole other tale to tell. Because a piece of wearable art is really a wearable story; the most interesting art always has something to say.

Pick up an object

Perhaps a shell, a toy, a recycled carton or a piece of food ... and think about these questions.

- What is it?
- What is it used for?
- What is it made from?
- Where would you normally get one?
- How did it find its way to you?

If it was three times the size of you, how would it make you feel? Would you laugh? Would you be scared?

If it was from an alien planet, what could its purpose be?

If you had a suit made from it, what could you do? What special powers could it give you?

If you had to explain the object to someone who couldn't see it, how would you describe it without using its name? What is its colour or texture like?

Be really descriptive. For instance, something might be yellow and smooth, but what else is yellow and smooth? Yellow like the summer sun and smooth as a Siamese cat; or yellow like tinned custard and smooth as the ocean on a calm day?

Go for a walk

Don't concentrate on getting somewhere, just on what is around you. The sights, the sounds – **and the smells!** What can you see? Pick up leaves and flower petals, sticks and stones. If they had been left by some mysterious creature, what had they been used for? Perhaps they were shedding skin and the petals aren't from flowers at all. What would a creature covered in petal skin look like? Would it be gentle or fierce?

Story time!

Copy these words down on separate bits of paper and put them into three bowls. Then with your eyes shut (no peeking!), choose one word from each category.

PERSON	THING	PLACE
queen	reptile	dream
dancer	animal	past
vampire	fruit	underwater
superhero	plant	legend
criminal	rock	future
king	insect	planet
soldier	bird	underworld
shape shifter	sea creature	castle
magician	alien	cyberspace
monster	skeleton	jungle

So...

You might have ended up with **queen**, **fruit** and **planet**. A Golden Queen peach from the planet Earth? Or a Queen from the planet Mars who finds it so hot and dusty there that she wears goggles and a hat made from cooler bags that she keeps her strawberry ice cream in? Which is the more interesting story to follow?

Put some new words in the bowls. Add to the list, make different combinations. See how many crazy ideas you can come up with.

Think about that object you looked at and described, or the things you saw on your walk. Could they be a part of your story?

Have you got an idea? Okay, let's draw it. What's that? You can't draw people? Well then, the next two pages are going to be very useful!

9

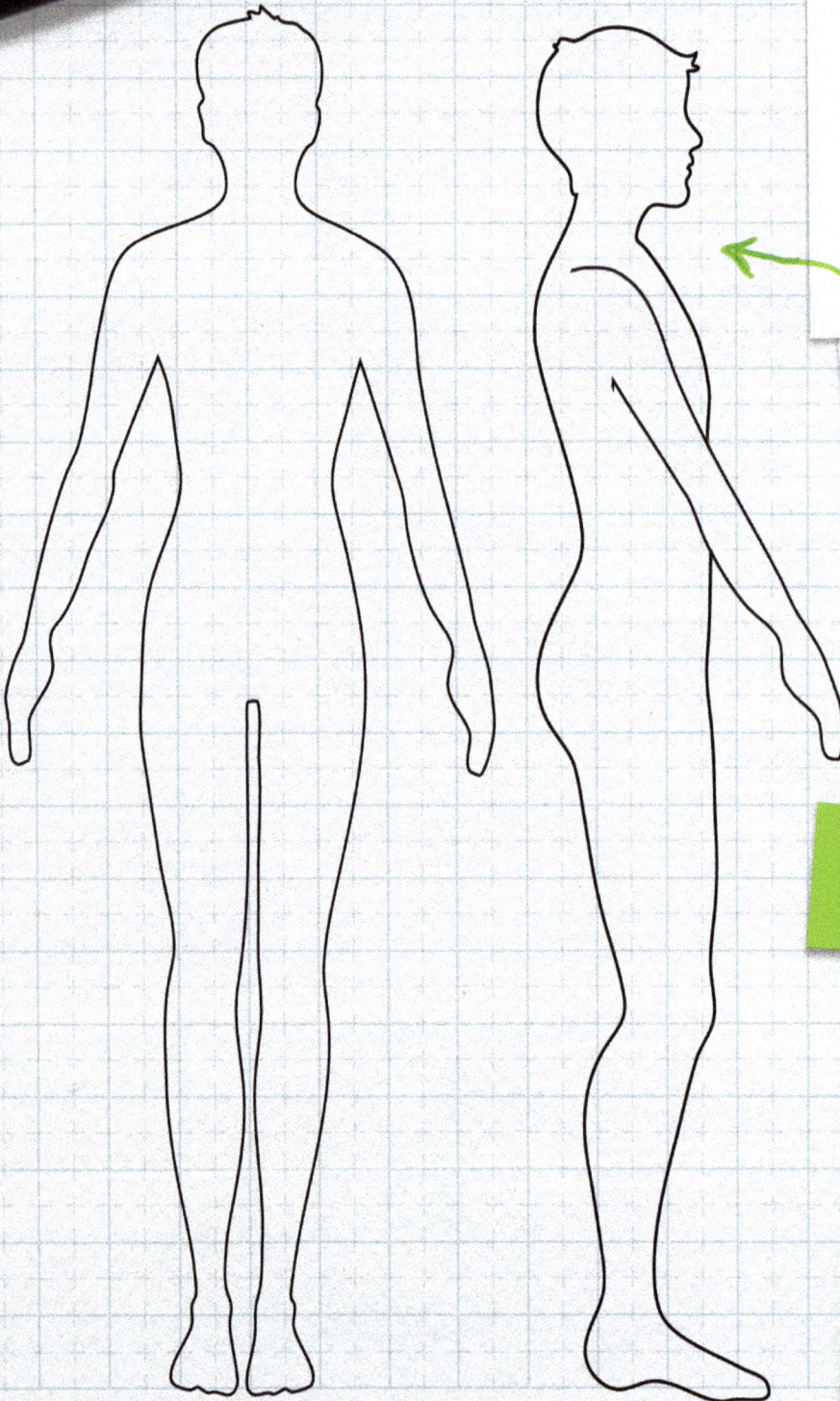

Sometimes it's hard to know what sort of shapes to use for your creations, so here are a few to photocopy or trace and try out.

Then, photocopy or trace these figures and see what exciting combinations you can build onto them.

What will stand out and tell your story?

This is way more fun than a dress!

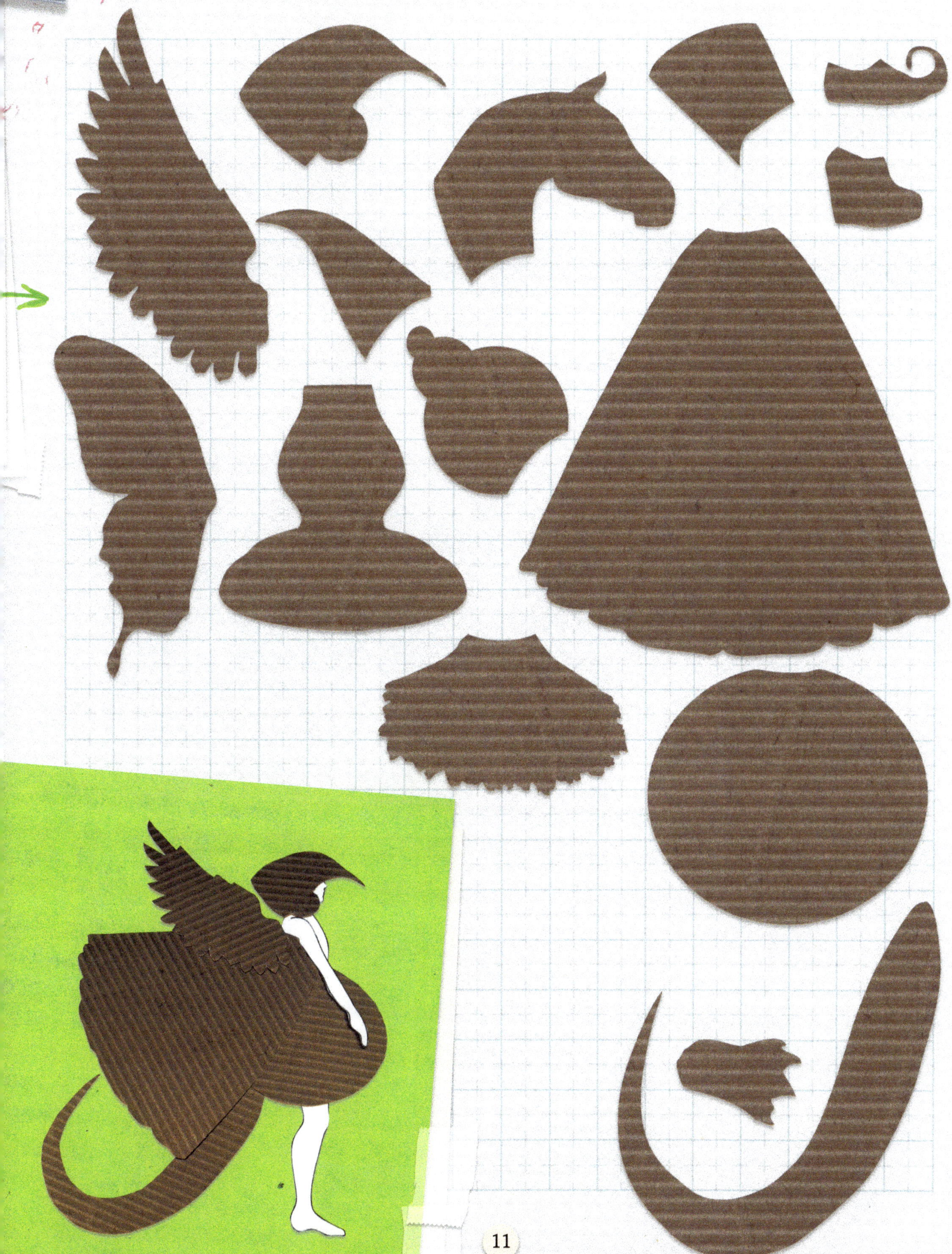

MAKE A MODEL

Making a mini model of your idea is really helpful. You can see how it might work on a real-sized person. This is a good way of figuring out how big different parts of the costume need to be and how many parts to it there should be. You can make models from cheap fashion dolls and dress them up in fabric and paper, but a cut-out shape is just as useful.

Trace the one on the opposite page and stick it onto card from a cereal box using a glue stick. Cut it out and bend the base around and tape or staple it into place.

YOU WILL NEED:

- thin card and paper
- glue
- scissors
- pencil or pen
- stapler or tape

Using a fashion figure doll works well.

1. Trace the outline onto paper and paste the paper onto card. Cut it out.

2. Bend at dotted lines.

3. Fold and staple or tape together at the back.

Mini Doll
Template

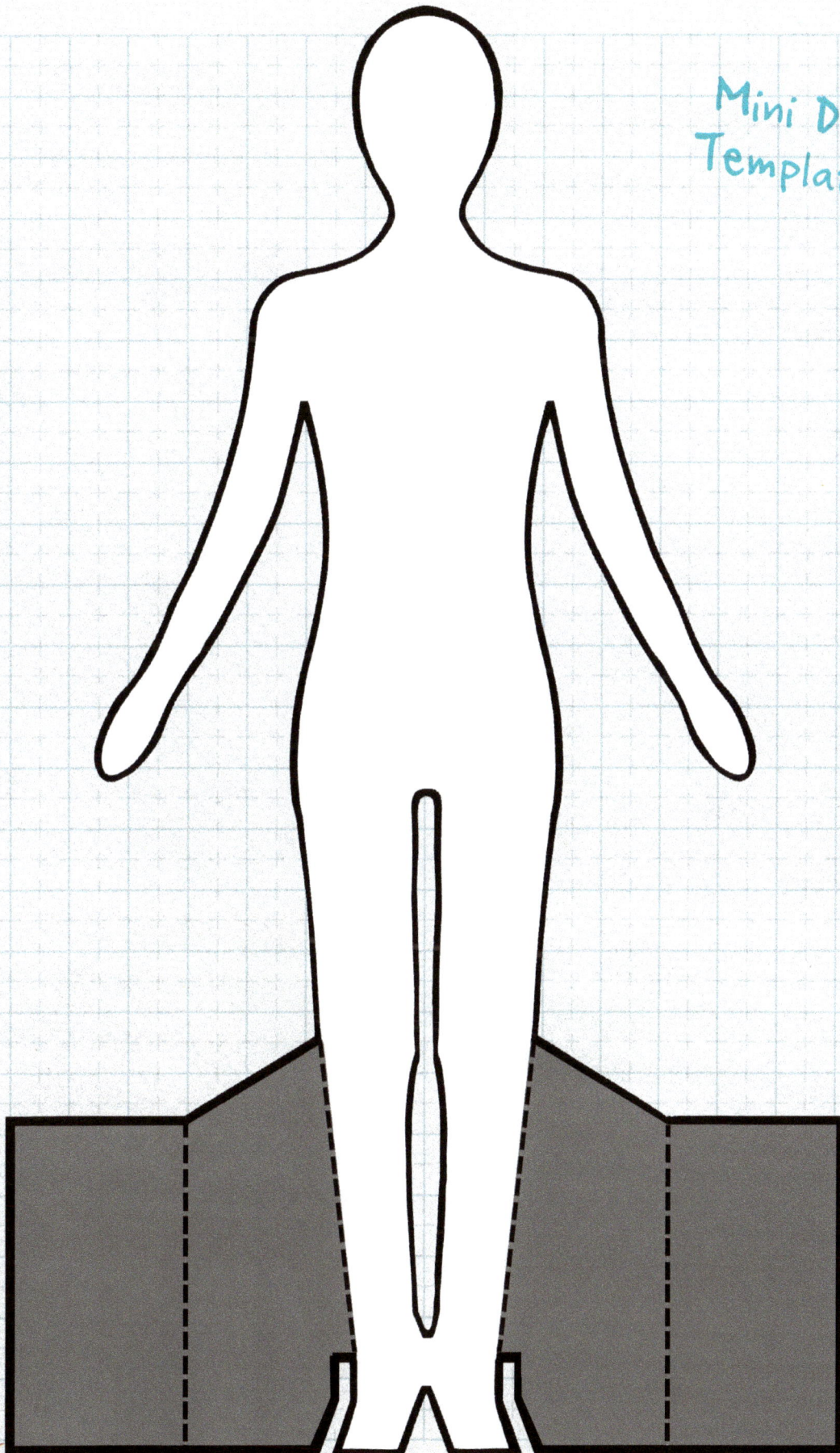

13

Now you can dress it up. Make the shapes you want out of scrap paper, plastic or fabric. Glue, tape or staple them on. Pipe cleaners, straws, string, skewers, doilies, wool and toothpicks are great for building too.

Think about the overall shape. If this was to be on a stage, how much room would it take up? Does it move in an interesting way? Do you need two people to manage it? Would it help to have wheels on it? Could you get a full-sized one up the stairs? Most importantly, does it help tell your story?

Some materials you could try.

Remember, you are just building a picture right now, not the finished garment. We will worry about how and what to make it out of soon. Right now, it's all about how it looks and what it does on the stage. A garment can do all kinds of things with a little help from the model and a few simple tricks ...

An example of a concept built with a cardboard mini doll.

14

ANIMATE!

Make it move

Little Girls should be seen and not heard.....

Life sized Victorian Porcelain 'doll'.

Underneath, the model wearing the doll like a backpack, starts the transformation

Lifts the skirt hem up and over her head in one dramatic fling.

New Millennium Girls — can do anything!

LOOK, NO HANDS!

If you have a costume with six arms, how do you make them move? Fishing line is the answer.

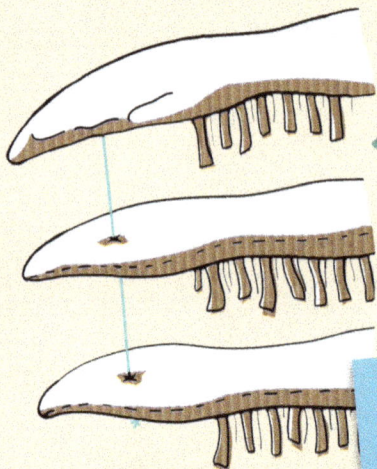

Suspend fake arms from gloved palms with fishing line, knotted at each stage. The fake arms will move with the real ones!

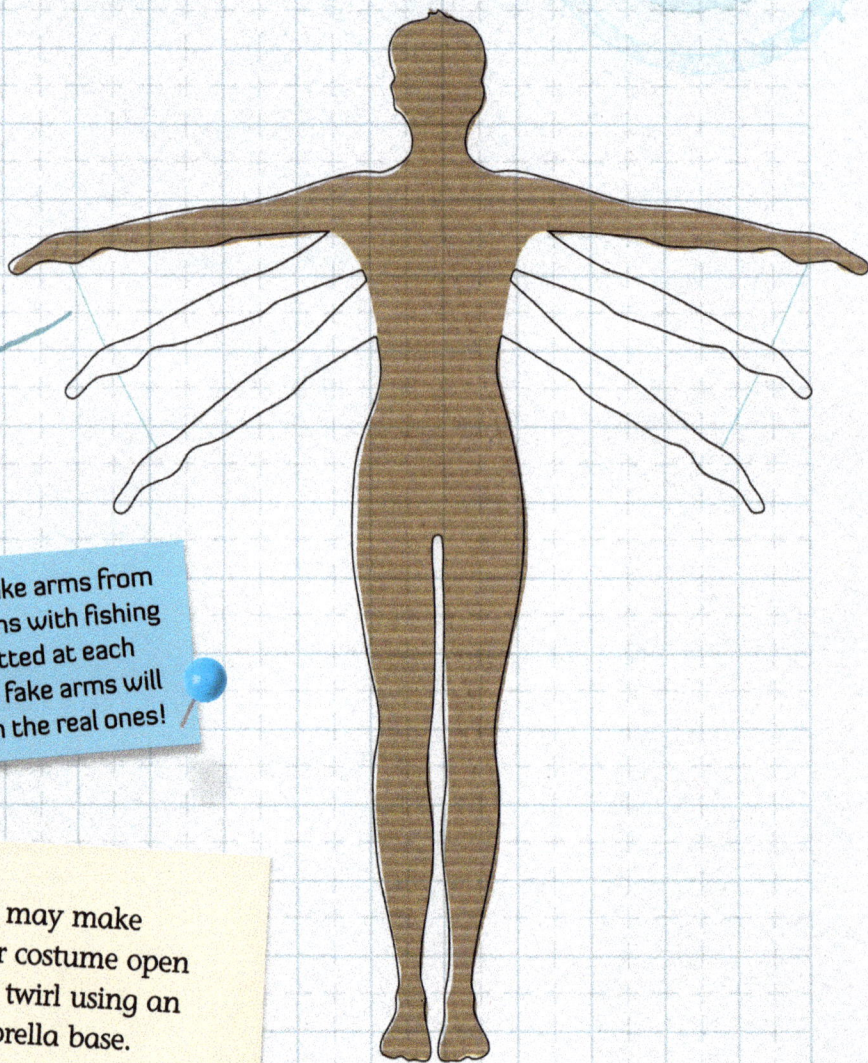

You may make your costume open and twirl using an umbrella base.

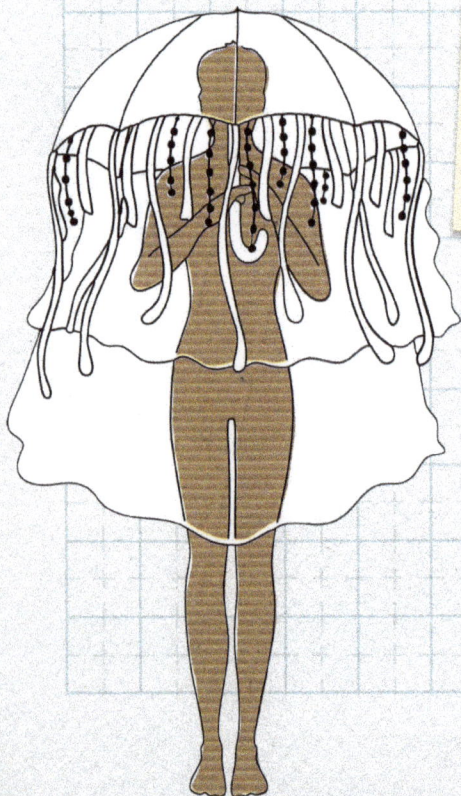

Long arms with moveable pincers? A plastic grabber animates your costume.

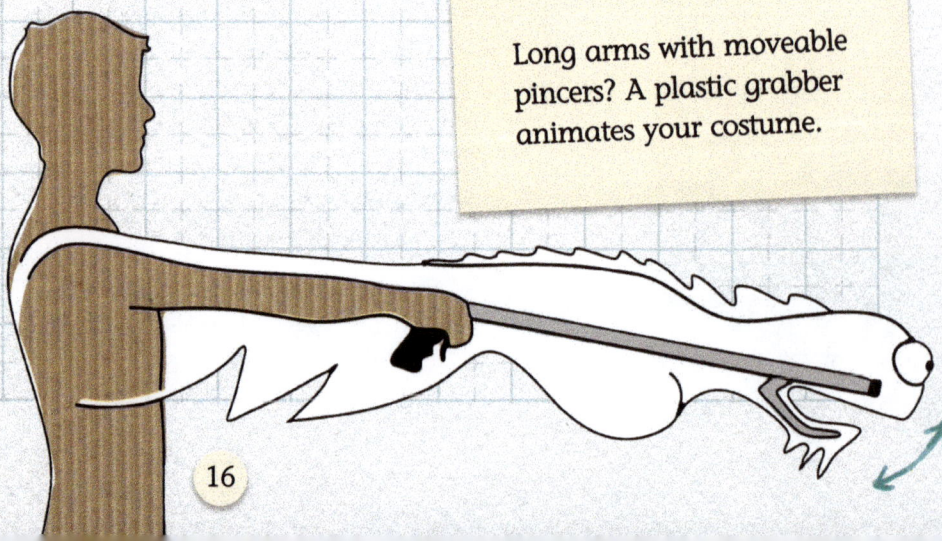

TRANSFORMATIONAL

Concealing and revealing are simple ways of giving a garment a bit of wow. You can do this effectively with capes and wings. The main thing to remember is that you want to create surprise.

What's underneath?

If you are creating large bird wings that open out, would you want to show a bird body? That would be expected. Show the unexpected instead. What do the wings hide?

Reveal your story!

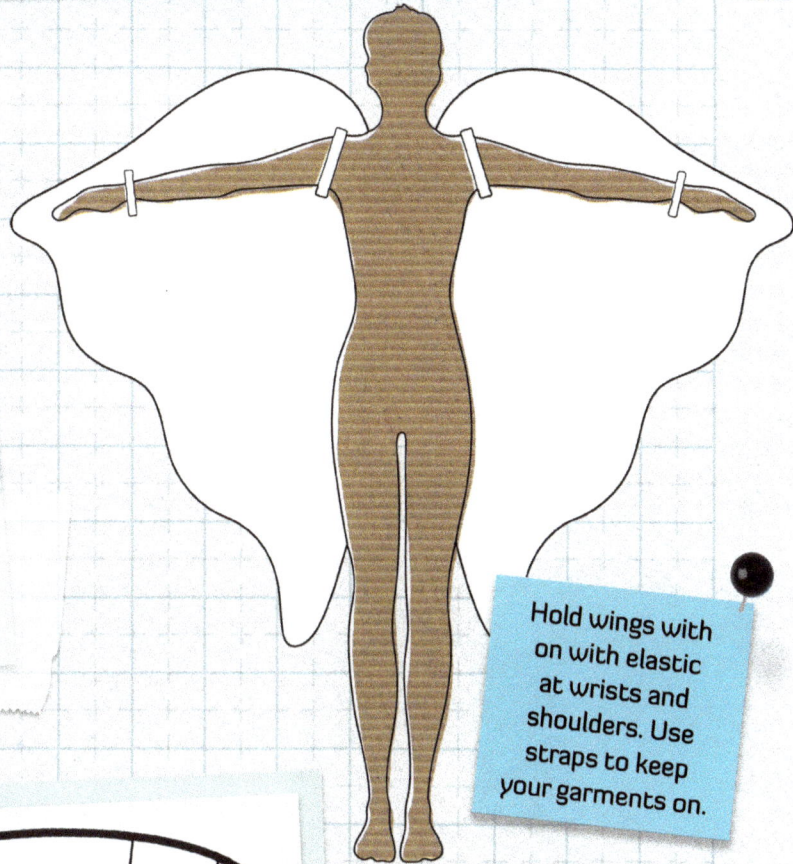

Hold wings with on with elastic at wrists and shoulders. Use straps to keep your garments on.

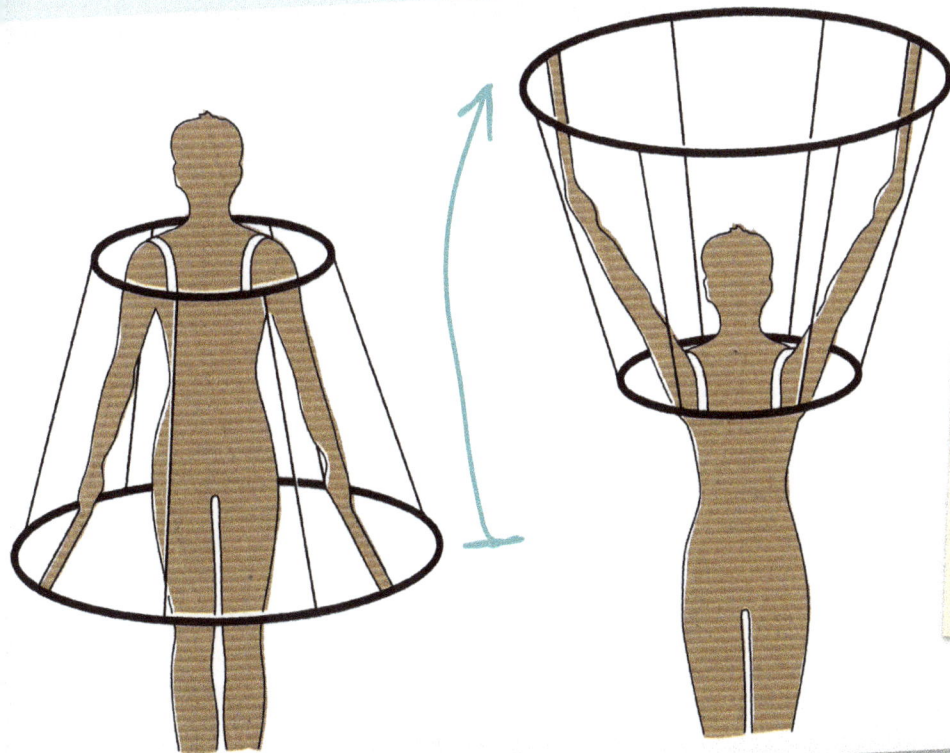

Can you make your garment turn inside out? This may be done using two different-sized hula hoops. What would you show on the inside?

PERSEPHONE IN CUBA ST.

Created by Fifi Colston

'Hades is like, such a drag, no wonder she's so Emo.'

I was watching a stylishly gothic Emo girl in Wellington's colourful Cuba Street. I wondered, 'Why is she so EMOtional? It's not like she has been married off to the Roman god of the Underworld at 15 and can only come up to play in the spring!' Then I thought, 'What if she was? What if she is the modern Persephone?'

This piece was created for the Illumination section of WOW using special fluoro materials and paints that show up under UV light. The stage is completely black and the model becomes invisible, with only the colours on the garment visible (as seen on the cover).

TIME TRAVELLING

*I've got a cool idea,
now what do I do?*

If you tell someone "I need a dragon alien costume out of sparkly fabric and sequins by tomorrow!" it will meet with a fire-breathing response. **Avoid stress** by planning your time and budget.

Budget:

MATERIALS REQUIRED	ESTIMATED COST	TO BE SOURCED FROM
fabric		
paper		
card		
plastic		
paint		
varnish		
glue		
tape		
thread		
zip		
Velcro		
cable ties		
wire		
mask base		
beads/buttons/sequins		
polyester stuffing		
make-up		
other items		
Total:		

What can you borrow or have donated to keep your costs down? Luckily the best wearable art is made from things found and recycled, and it's amazing how far you can get by asking people nicely.

Where could you get some of these things? Could you ask the parents from school to donate bits of fabric they don't want? The school newsletter is a good way to put out a request. Has your school got paper, glue, tape and paints you can use? If you asked a local fabric, stationery or hardware store for any leftover paints or materials you might be surprised by how helpful they are.

Go into the store, introduce yourself and ask to speak to the manager. Show them your project, your drawings and model. Say what you need to make it and ask if they can help in any way. Offer to make them an official sponsor! Invite them to the show and send them a certificate of appreciation.

Other great places to find cheap materials are charity shops or recycling stores at refuse stations.

Now you know what your budget is, you need to track where the time goes, because it can really disappear fast, and you want a really wonderful finished garment to show on stage. Look at the tasks and the people involved. It helps to begin with the end date first and work backwards from there.

Be realistic about time. Papier-mâché, for instance, will take more than a day to dry before you can paint it, and you need to allow time for things to go wrong! It's easy to waste time in the first days or weeks, then find you are very short of time in the last few days before the performance.

Things to do:

TASKS	TEAM/PEOPLE	DUE DATE	COMPLETED?
Brainstorm			
Sketches			
Mock-up			
Pattern making			
Find materials			
Trial techniques			
Choose a model			
Cut pattern pieces			
1st fitting with paper mock			
Construction			
2nd fitting			
Painting			
3rd fitting			
Make a box or hanger for the garment			
Choose music			
Choreography			
Props (do you need some?)			
Lighting and technical			
Photography (of the garment)			
Dress rehearsal			
Performance			
Celebration of a job well done!			

Use the calendar below as a guide to plan your weeks. Photocopy (and trim) this page as many times as you need and pin them in a place where you can see them easily.

Write the date in the left-hand corner of each box. From your task sheet, write on the calendar when things need to be done by.

Planner:

	MONDAY	TUESDAY	WEDNESDAY	THURSDAY	FRIDAY	SATURDAY	SUNDAY
WEEK 1							
WEEK 2							
WEEK 3							
WEEK 4							

TOOLS OF THE TRADE

Before you do
anything else,
you need a toolkit

BASIC TOOLS

Scissors

A good pair of scissors is vital; but which sort should you have? It's a good idea to have two pairs. Have one really good, sharp pair for cutting *fabric only*, and do not use them for cutting anything else, not even paper! Write 'Fabric' on the handles so you remember. Other, cheaper scissors are fine for all the other things you want to cut. A small pair is handy to cut fiddly things.

Needles and pins

Pins hold stuff in place before you sew or glue it. Use ones with bright-coloured heads on them so you can find them easily. Long florist pins are very useful too. A set of sewing needles in different sizes should be part of your toolkit. Craft needles have big 'eyes' on them, good for threading thick wool. If you have access to a sewing machine, ask for some lessons. Machine sewing makes fabric stay put!

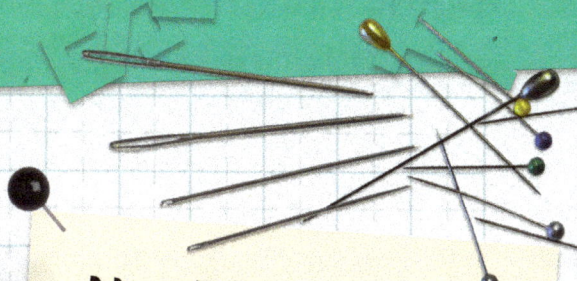

Craft Knife

A really sharp craft knife is an essential part of your toolkit. Don't buy one of those cheap packs of 20 craft knives. The handles are wobbly and made from thin plastic and may break when you use them. Get a good brand with lots of spare blades. The worst craft knife accidents happen when you use a blunt blade because you have to use too much pressure to make a cut and, if the knife slips ... well, you'd better have a first aid kit handy.

Cutting mat

Always use one when cutting anything with a craft knife. You can buy them at art, craft and stationery stores, or use a thick piece of cardboard, hardboard or a plastic kitchen bread board.

Paintbrushes

There are a huge variety of paintbrushes and you don't have to use really expensive ones; in fact cheaper ones are often better. Stiff bristle brushes are great for texture. A 50 mm house painting brush is good for covering big areas. If you are doing any fine detail then get a synthetic 'round' brush and a flat one too. The only brushes to avoid are the ones meant for little kids that cost almost nothing; they are useless and you'd be better off saving your money.

The main thing to remember is to wash your brushes properly after use and leave them to dry. Never leave their bristles sitting in a jar of water or on a plate with paint all over them.

Chipped plates, bowls, clean glass jars and plastic takeaway boxes make useful paint and water containers. Worn-out cotton T-shirts, towels and pillowcases can be cut up and recycled into paint rags. Old sheets make great drop cloths to protect surfaces where you are working. Keep an old shirt handy to wear over your good clothes.

Pliers

'Rat-nosed' pliers are the most useful sort to have; they are great for pulling and bending bits of wire. A pair of side cutters make a good companion to the pliers too; nifty for snipping.

Side cutters

Rat-nosed pliers

Protective mask

If you are using any sprays at all, or sanding things and raising a lot of dust, you **MUST** wear a mask. There are lots of disposable ones you can get at a hardware store.

If you take care of a nice brush it will be with you for years; just like a good friend!

Tape is most useful in the early stages of your creation: holding things together and creating shapes that can then be glued, painted or covered in paper or fabric.

So, what kind of tape do you need?

Double sided tape

Great for holding plastic and paper together.

Masking tape

Probably the most useful art and craft tape. It wraps around most things and holds them in place. You can remove it easily or paint over it.

Duct tape or Gaffer

This is really sticky and has a woven fabric base to it. It's strong and is excellent for holding cardboard or plastic constructions together. To cut it, you don't need scissors as you can just rip it. You can paint over it too.

Clear sticky tape

Very handy for paper and plastic. Finding the end can be tricky so if you don't have a tape dispenser, fold back a small piece of tape when you finish using it, or stick a paper clip under the end.

Electrical tape

This is plastic based and comes in lots of bright colours. It's fun to wrap around wire shapes, pulling and stretching it as you go.

There are all kinds of glue but most of them aren't useful for your craft work. Superglue bonds your fingers together and not much else, Gorilla glue is just like really thick PVA, and a glue stick will only hold your pictures together. The following glue types are the best for your Wearable Wonder.

Draw pictures with a hot-glue gun, then paint the cooled-down result!

Hot-glue gun

Probably the most useful thing you'll ever own. You can buy them at art & craft, stationery and hardware stores. The small ones are easiest to use and you have a choice between low- and high-temperature ones. High-temp glue is stronger but you do have to be very careful not to burn yourself. You'll need lots of hot-glue sticks, so get a big pack. A hot-glue gun is awesome for creating texture and decoration as well as sticking things together. Hot glue will stick plastic and foam together, but can also melt it. Don't use it on polystyrene unless you want big holes in it!

PVA glue

Also known as white glue, wood glue, Elmers glue or craft glue. It's all the same and it's cheaper at a hardware store. Great for wood, paper and fabric, but it won't stick polystyrene or tin. If you dilute it with water, it makes a good cheap varnish.

Clear glue

This dries crystal clear and is quite flexible. Perfect for gluing on small fake jewels and anything lightweight.

Contact adhesives

These are the sort that you spread a little on each surface, wait for it to dry and then clamp them together. They make really strong bonds and are perfect for foam rubber and thick fabrics. They also melt polystyrene and are very smelly, so you need to take lots of care when using them.

Epoxy glue

Expoxy comes in two parts that you need to mix in equal amounts. It is very fast setting and really strong. It's the best glue for tin, hard plastic and things that just won't hold together with other glues. Expensive and smelly; use it only when nothing else has worked.

Spray glue

This is useful for bonding two thin flat surfaces together where you don't want any lumps or bumps. It's also good at sticking your lungs together so use it very carefully, outside and with a protective mask.

Wallpaper paste

This is cheap and comes as a powder from a hardware store. Follow the instructions on the packet; you only need a small amount in a large container of water to make heaps of glue. This is great for papier-mâché.

29

OTHER USEFUL THINGS

... to have in your toolkit

- safety pins in different sizes
- thread
- string
- fishing line
- a metal skewer for making holes
- plastic clothes pegs for holding things while glue is setting
- a pencil
- a stapler
- latex gloves

A plastic table cloth or a few plastic bags cut open and taped together to make a sheet is excellent for keeping your work surface clean and dry.

When you have gathered together all these things, find a box to keep them in. It doesn't matter if it's a cardboard one, a plastic one or a fancy builder's one, just so long as it has your name on it and a big 'Hands Off' notice on it! After all, you are going to need these things to create your artwork.

Now ... what will you make it from?

MATERIALS

What to look for and where to find it

You might have found something you want to make a Wearable Wonder out of: some packaging that got thrown out at a nearby store, a pile of CDs that no one uses any more, or a bunch of socks that have lost their partners. Or you might be wondering what else you can find cheaply to turn into your creation.

Let's search them out!

The best tins to use are the ones that have a pull-top lid as they come away nice and clean, with a safe edge.

And remember, anything that is **hazardous waste,** like batteries or machine oil, **cannot be used** either. If you are not sure if you should use it, ask someone who will know.

Recyclables

Newspapers, envelopes, junk mail, wrappers, cereal boxes, egg cartons, takeaway coffee cups, soft drink bottles, supermarket bags, margarine and yogurt containers, ice cream tubs, bread bags, tie tags, milk bottles, lids, bubble wrap, polystyrene, tin foil, jar lids, tin cans, screw top caps, drink cans...

What recycling can't you use for your Wearable Wonder?

Glass is definitely out. It can break – and broken glass cuts people. Put any glass bottles and jars in a box for the recycling collection, along with the lids from opened tin cans, as they are too sharp and jagged to use for your costume. The tins themselves are fine if you make sure the edge has a rim on it and is smooth. If it is sharp, don't use it! Safety for your model is very important.

Clean and dry everything before you use it.

These Steam Punk goggles were made from takeout coffee cups, biscuit packaging, fur, leather and tin scraps, and holographic plastic.

Up-cycling

When your plastic, glass, cans and paper go to the recycling depot, they get turned into new forms of what they used to be: plastic gets shredded and made into new bottles and containers, glass gets crushed and made into new glass bottles, tins get melted down and made into new cans.

What you can do with some of your recycling is make new and useful objects. This is called up-cycling. Take things you might otherwise throw away, cut, shape, paint and decorate them, and create wearable art.

Over the next few pages we'll look at how you can do that with things from your recycling bin.

FANTASTIC PLASTIC

Soft drink bottles

Plastic bottles make great accessories. They can be cut with scissors, and held together with tape and/or a little hot glue (not too much because it will melt the bottle.)

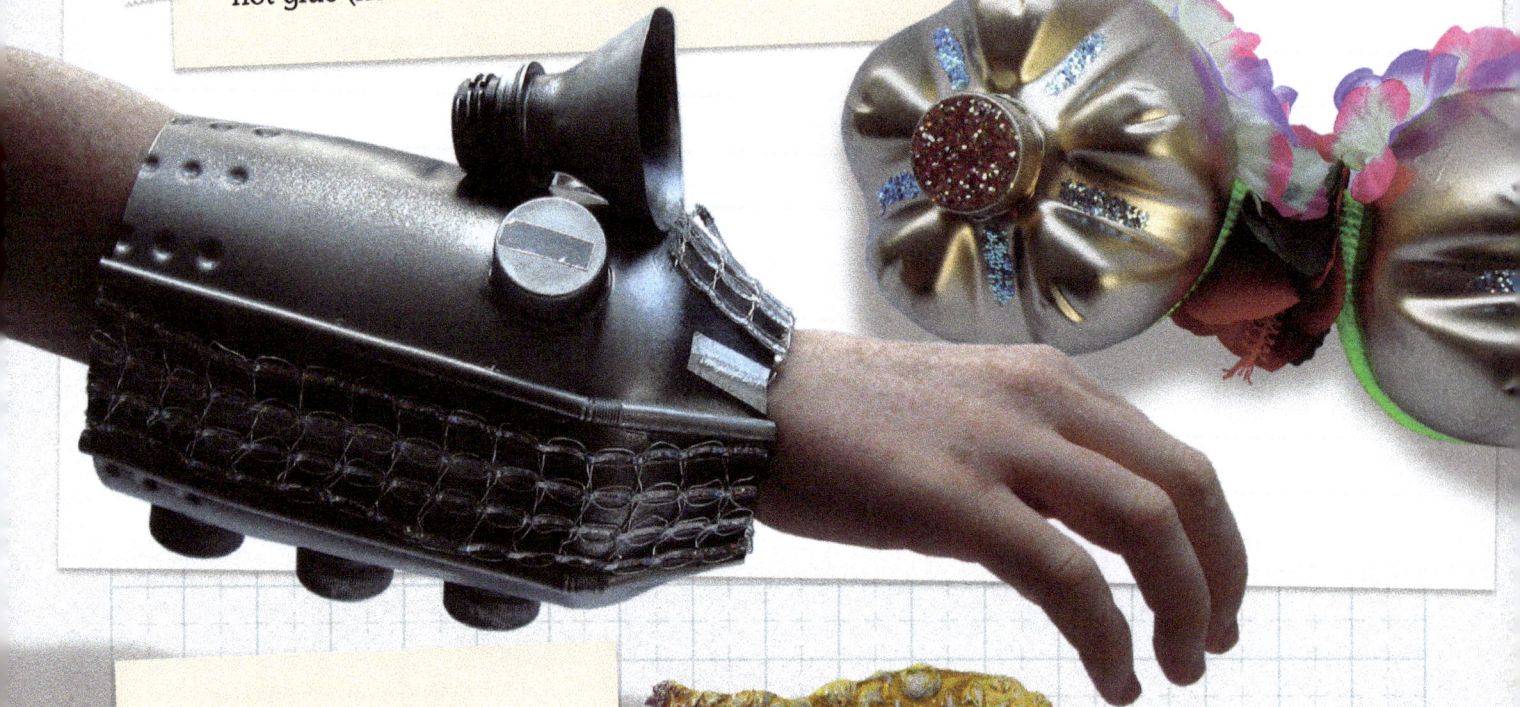

Bubble wrap

This makes lightweight constructions with a wonderful texture that can be painted. Use clear tape and double sided tape to hold it together.

A light coat of polyurethane spray sealer will stop paint flaking off.

Woven strips

These are not only decorative but very strong. Use packing ties or lengths cut from ice cream tubs, old tarpaulins or plastic bags. Hold the edges together with duct tape.

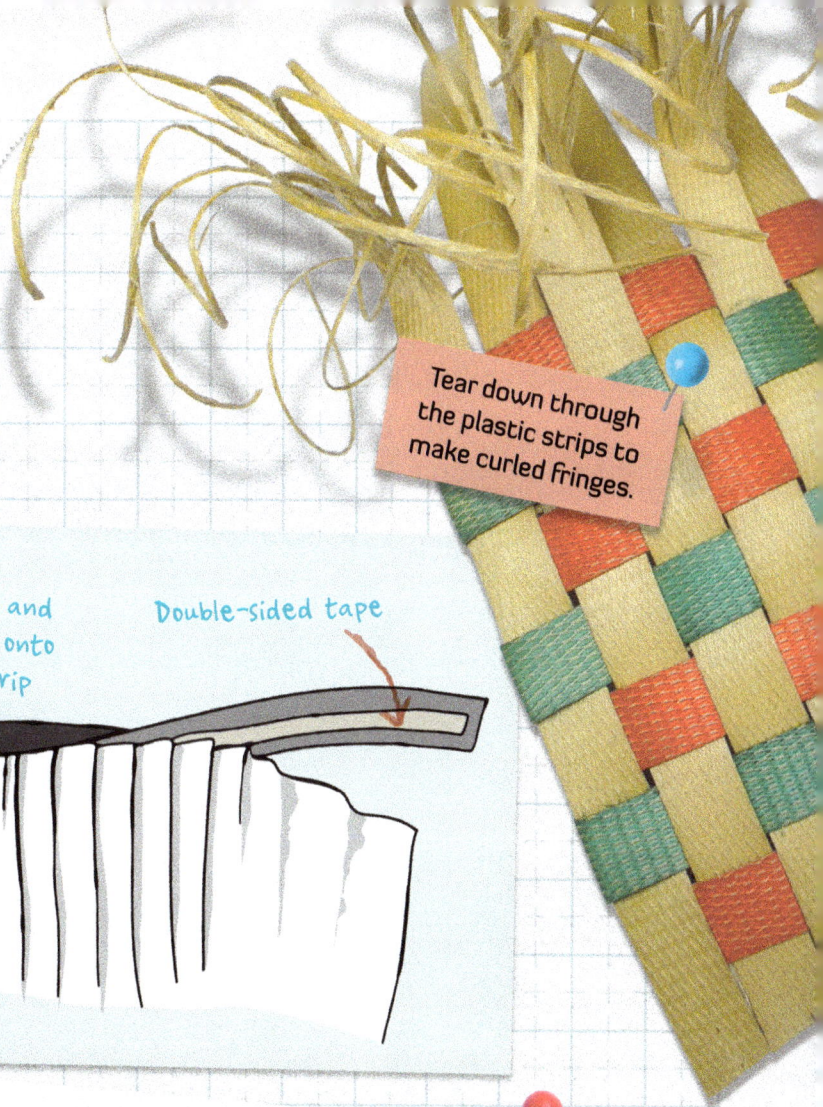

Tear down through the plastic strips to make curled fringes.

Plastic bags

Plastic supermarket bags and black bin liners make great skirts, capes and flowers. Clear and double-sided tape hold everything in place.

Fold pleats and tape them onto a plastic strip

Double-sided tape

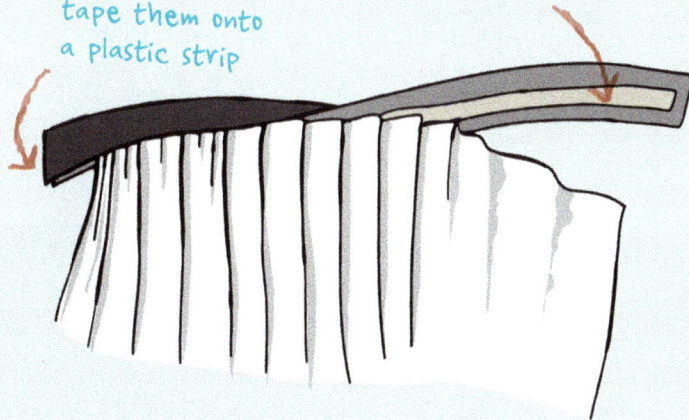

How to make a plastic bag flower

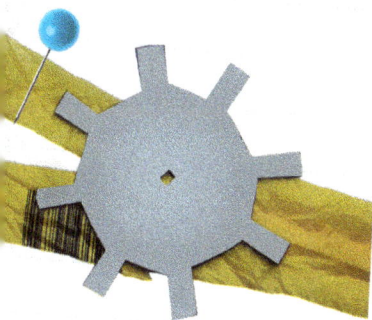

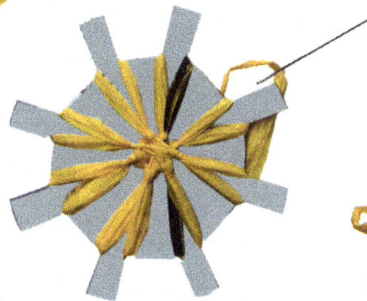

① Make the daisy loom by cutting it out of an ice cream tub lid and make a hole in the middle. Flatten out a plastic shopping bag and cut it into 2cm wide strips lengthways.

② Thread a strip onto a craft needle and sew it through the hole leaving 5cm dangling. Now loop the strip around a spoke, down and around the opposite one and so on until you have all the spokes wrapped.

③ Pass the needle under the centre strips and sew around each petal until you have secured them all in place.

④ Pass the needle back through the middle and tie the two ends together. Slip the daisy off the spokes, then pull it off the loom. Fluff the petals out if you like a fuller flower.

THE PAPER WORLD

Egg cartons, coffee cups and trays, paper plates, cardboard boxes, doilies, brown paper bags, corrugated card, packaging, building paper ... so many paper things we use and throw away each day, just waiting to be made into art!

Egg cartons are made from recycled paper and they are so much fun to glue and paint.

Egg cartons also make the best paper mash!

MIGHTY MASH

There is a bit of an art to making really effective papier-mâché. Try this method for a really mighty mash!

YOU WILL NEED:

- egg cartons
- a bucket
- boiling water
- a blender/food processor (ask first!)
- wallpaper paste or diluted PVA glue

1

Tear up your egg cartons into postage stamp sized pieces and put them in a bucket. Then pour boiling water over them so that they are only just covered and leave them to soak for a couple of days. Stir every so often so they are well soaked, and pull them apart a bit more with your hands.

2

Once they are really mushy, put through a blender with a little of the liquid, a cupful at a time, until the mix is as smooth as you can get it (it will still be a bit lumpy). If you don't have a blender or food processor, use a potato masher and your hands to break up the pulp.

3

Mix up about a cupful of wallpaper paste. (If you use PVA glue, water it down a little.) Mix it into the paper pulp. Don't make the mixture too sloppy; it should be the consistency of soft biscuit dough. Now it is ready to use.

5

When it is properly dried out, paint it. For extra finish, a coat of clear varnish or watered down PVA glue will seal it.

4

Line a plate or cover a board with a plastic bag and build whatever you like. Remember, the thicker the mash, the longer it will take to dry. Leave your finished piece beside a column heater or put it in the hot water cupboard to dry. It will take about 3–4 days, or less in the summer sunshine.

Reshape it

Paper can be crumpled, folded and pleated to make all kinds of wonderful shapes.

Seal the surface of your collage (also called découpage) with water-based varnish.

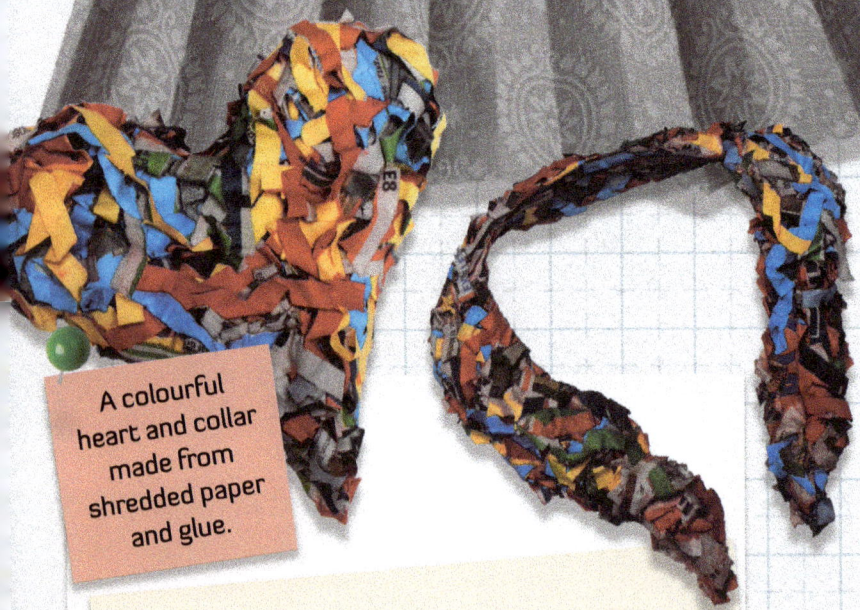

A colourful heart and collar made from shredded paper and glue.

If you want to create amazing texture, layer papers and card with glue. Tear, cut, crumple and squash it. If you put it through an office paper shredder and add a little wallpaper paste to it, you can make a wonderful, colourful sculpture.

And don't forget collage: cut out pictures from old magazines, cards and wrapping papers to glue onto the surface.

A COMPLETE FABRICATION

There are all kinds of fabric with different uses. Knowing what to use is the trick, so let's have a look at some different kinds and what they are good for:

Cotton

Natural, used for things like sheets, towels, T-shirts and jeans. Easy to sew, takes paint and dye. Frays and doesn't melt with heat. An old sheet is great for making things out of.

Polyester and polar fleece

Synthetic, used for things like upholstery, mats, blankets, duvets and cheap clothing. Doesn't take dye, but you can paint it. Doesn't fray, melts with heat. Cheap.

Felt

Natural, used for things like hats, bags, drawer linings and craft projects. Doesn't fray, comes in bright colours. You need to dye it in hot water. Easy to sew and great for shape and texture.

Lycra

Synthetic, used for things like leggings, swimsuits and dance leotards. Stretchy, hard to dye or paint. Doesn't fray; you can make great textures by stretching and heating it.

Silk

Natural, used for things like shirts, ties, slips, dresses, kimonos and parachutes. Really light, sometimes see-through, takes dye and paint really well. Doesn't fray much. Expensive!

Satin

Synthetic or natural, shiny and used for luxury sheets, fancy dresses and sleepwear. Frays and is slippery to sew. Mostly dyes in hot water. Expensive, but pretty.

Tulle, net and organza

Mostly synthetic, see-through and easy to hand sew. Great for creating things that need to flutter in the breeze, look like clouds or mist.

Frost cloth

Synthetic, thin, white, and made from polyester – used for putting over plants to protect them in the winter. It's also awesome for making bird wings and all sorts of things. You can buy it at hardware and garden stores. You can sew it, glue it, tape it and paint it.

Shade cloth

Synthetic, like frost cloth but black. Great for making capes and bat wings.

Fake fur

Synthetic and expensive. Look out for old Santa hats and toys to take apart.

Muslin

Natural, cotton-based, very fine and light. Cheap and very easy to hand sew and dye.

Hessian

Natural, easy to dye and sew, and to weave other yarns into.

Canvas

Natural, thick, and great for painting on. That's why artists use it!

Wool

Natural and comes in all kinds of woven types. The most useful for costume are old blankets, which dye really well, don't fray, are easy to sew and fantastic to create texture and sculpture with.

FABRIC TO DYE FOR!

Dyeing fabric is very tricky if you don't have a big enough container, so use a child's paddling pool, plastic rubbish bin or large storage box. Do it outside so you won't get dye all over the floor! Wear OLD clothes and rubber gloves and put down a tarpaulin or big sheet beneath the container.

You can use watered down acrylic paint instead of special fabric dyes. It's much cheaper, and as long as you aren't planning to wash your Wearable Wonder afterwards, paint is just fine. The dyes you use for art at school are perfect too.

Not washing your garment afterwards means you don't have to bother adding tons of salt, which sets the colour with fabric dye.

Dyes always take to the fabric best if you wet it first and have the dye warm. Make sure you have somewhere to dry the fabric – hang it off a washing line and let it drip. Dyeing is a fine day activity!

Instead of just soaking the whole piece of material in a tub, try these dyeing methods:

Dip-dyeing

Wet the whole piece then dip just the bottom edge in the dye. Let it soak up through the fabric to create a graduated colour.

This old bed sheet and piece of muslin were dyed with paint to make an 'under the sea' garment.

Tie-dyeing

Tie string tightly around parts of your fabric before dipping it. When it is dry, untie the string and see what patterns you've made.

Scrunching

Scrunch up the fabric and dip parts into the dye or brush the dye over the surface. Smooth it out and let it dry.

Flick-dyeing

Lay the fabric on the ground and flick dye onto it with a thick brush. A cheap plastic spray bottle does a good job of spattering colour too.

Layering

Dip the whole piece of fabric, let it dry. Then tie-dye it in another colour. Scrunch it, flick it and build up layers of colour. Work from light colours to dark.

A BIT DISTRESSED!

Distressing is when you take a piece of fabric and make it look dirty, rough or broken. This is a useful when you want to make something look really old and worn. There are lots of different ways to do this without rubbing mud onto it.

Bleaching

Ordinary household bleach is great for taking colour out of dyed fabrics. It will also take colour out of your clothes and it's not good on your skin. If you want to use it follow these instructions carefully.

Have an adult supervise. As with dyeing fabric, wear OLD clothes and rubber gloves and put down a tarpaulin or big sheet – outdoors. Make sure all animals and little brothers and sisters are safely out of the way. Bleach is a poison and you must take care.

Half fill a jar or bottle with water and the rest with bleach. This will be plenty strong enough. You can paint or flick it onto your fabric with a brush. It will take out colour wherever it lands, so take care with the surroundings. Bathroom mould remover is just bleach in a spray bottle. This works well too.

Bleach does not work on polyester, lycra and other synthetic materials, so don't even try.

This cloak has had bleach brushed through a stencil to create a flower pattern.

Bleach is a poison and you must take care. Use your protective mask.

You can never tell exactly how bleaching will turn out - that's part of the fun!

43

Heating

Some synthetic materials distort with heat. A hairdryer on its hottest setting can pucker the material and make it look like alien skin. Be careful not to overheat the hairdryer by holding it too close to the fabric; it will stop working. If you have access to a heat gun, the sort that is used for stripping paint, you can use that too – but be very careful not to burn both yourself and the fabric.

Fraying

Some fabrics fray really well. It's easy, just pull loose threads out. Try snipping tiny holes in the fabric and fray the edges.

Grating

Yep, use a kitchen grater! Scrunch your fabric up and rub it against the fine grating side. This is especially good for woollen materials. It will snag and roughen the nicest of fabrics and make them look like they've been on a mountainous quest.

Ripping

Tear and rip your fabric to get rough edges. Cotton and silk rip best.

Moulding

Fine cottons and silk can be made into rock-hard sculptures.

(1) Lay a plastic sheet on a flat surface, then water down PVA glue in a bowl so it looks like full cream, not skinny, milk.

(2) Dip your fabric into it and make sure it's completely soaked. Hold it up and let the excess drip off (squeeze it between your fingers to get rid of the really drippy bits).

(3) Lay it on the plastic, crumple it, make it into shapes. Or you can lay it over things like an orange or a bowl covered in cling film (so it doesn't stick). Use pegs to hold the shapes in place. Let it dry overnight.

(4) When you lift it up off the plastic the fabric will be solid and ready to use. Moulded fabric can be painted too.

Stitching

A needle and thread creates great texture. Make large running stitches then pull them tight. Make bubbles and bobbles in random places. Does it look like something from the forest floor or a reptile zoo? Use different colours and thickness of thread and wool to add interest.

Stretching

Lycra and knit fabric will stretch over things and, if you secure it well, it can look very cool. Try stretching the fabric over different things. See how it alters what they might be.

This metallic lycra was stretched over foam circles to make red blood cells for a dress.

45

Foam is a strong and useful building material and it helps to know which kind to use.

Foam rubber

This comes in different thicknesses and is the sort that is used for topper pads and seat cushions. If someone will donate you an old topper pad, you can make it go a long way. Cut and shape it with a craft or kitchen knife. Glue it together with contact adhesive. Makes lightweight bulky things. Best covered with fabric but you can paint it if you want something more textured.

EVA foam

This is what's called high density foam; it is very smooth and you will probably recognise it as a bed roll for camping, most often in blue or green. It is the best foam for construction because you can glue it (hot glue gun or contact adhesive), shape it with heat, cut it and paint it – and it's very light and hardwearing.

A hot soldering iron was used to melt the decoration into the foam for this giant crab claw.

Expander foam

Builders use this to plug up holes, but it makes really clever stuff in the hands of an artist. It isn't cheap but a single can goes a long way. Use your protective mask and rubber gloves. Shake it up, spray it onto your base … then see what happens. It expands! After 24 hours you can chop into it, shape it and paint it.

Cream for a pavlova hat will never melt when made from foam!

Polystyrene

There are many types of this but the one you'll be most familiar with is the white foam packaging that comes around an appliance. It is very useful for building things because it is so light and you can cut it with a craft or kitchen knife or fine hacksaw. It makes a bit of a mess because little bits of it get everywhere, so keep a vacuum cleaner handy. It is tricky to glue because you need special polystyrene cement, but duct tape will hold it together and you can pin pieces with toothpicks and bamboo skewers. It paints up really well.

These polystyrene 'rocks' won't weigh your garment down.

ALL THE OTHER STUFF

Sometimes you just need a filler – something to pad out your creation.

Here are some things you can use:

Dacron

This fluffy cushion and soft toy filler comes in a bag and you can buy it at craft and fabric stores. Or go to a charity shop and look for cheap pillows and cushions that you can take apart for the filling.

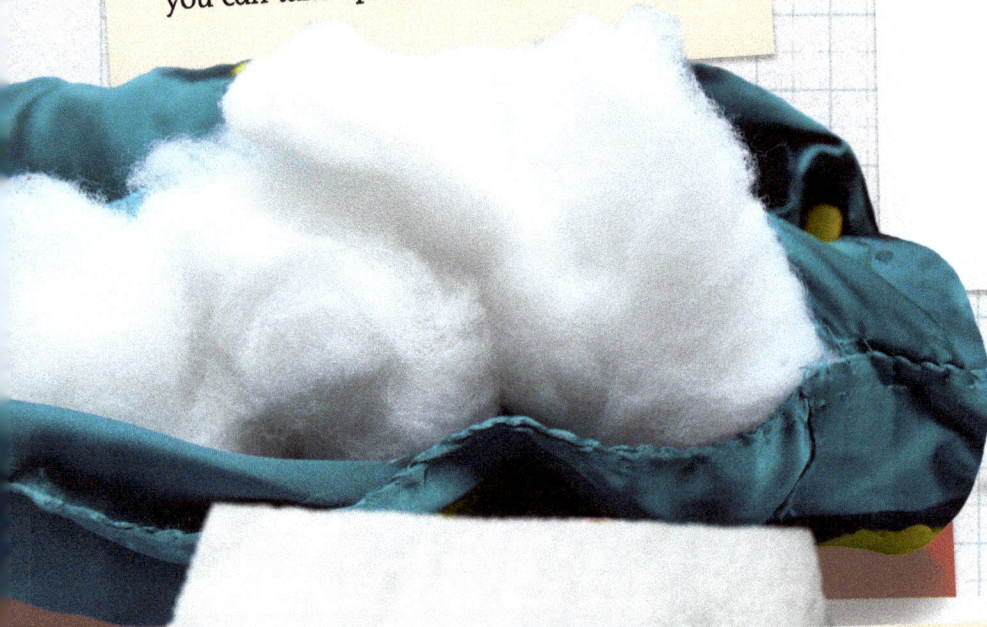

Shredded paper

Make filling out of newspaper, junk mail and old letters by putting it through an office paper shredder. Lots of fun!

Wadding or polyester fibre

Like Dacron but comes in a roll, is flat and thick and you can cut it.

NATURALLY YOURS

Go for a walk on the beach, by the lake, in the bush, in the garden or in the park. See what you can find. The beach has shells, dried seaweed, driftwood and pumice. The garden, bush and parks have fallen leaves, twigs, seed heads, pinecones and harakeke (flax). Both places have bird feathers!

But there are other places you can look for natural materials too. Builders' yards have lots of curly wood shavings. The pantry and supermarket have wooden ice block sticks, bamboo skewers, seeds and beans. Craft shops sell willow and cane. Stationery shops have recycled paper twist.

Leather

Scraps of leather are great. If it is thin enough you can stretch it around shapes. Glue leather with contact adhesive.

Sheep's wool

Unspun wool is great for felting. Put old towels over your work area and cover with bubble wrap. Lay bits of wool on top and gently pour hot, soapy water over them. Cover with another sheet of bubble wrap, roll it up in the towel and roll it back and forth several times until the fibres combine to make felt. Take off the top layer of bubble wrap and let it dry.

Fun felt pixie hats made by Jean Burgers from Wellington.

Feathers

Delicate and light for decoration. Glue or sew them into place.

Pumice

Find it on beaches or lakesides. Easy to carve and small pieces make good natural beads.

Shells

There are so many sorts and those you find on the beach often already have holes in them – very handy for sewing onto your costume.

Leaves

Glue dried leaves onto your artwork. They need to be sealed first with varnish (PVA) to stop them cracking and falling off.

Seeds

The bulk bins at the supermarket have all kinds of dried seeds and beans, ready for glueing into place. Use PVA or clear glue to create patterns.

Bone

Easy to find after dinner! Collect meat or chicken bones from a roast or casserole and boil them for a few hours to get all the meat and fat off. Leave them to dry out completely before using, then weave them into your art.

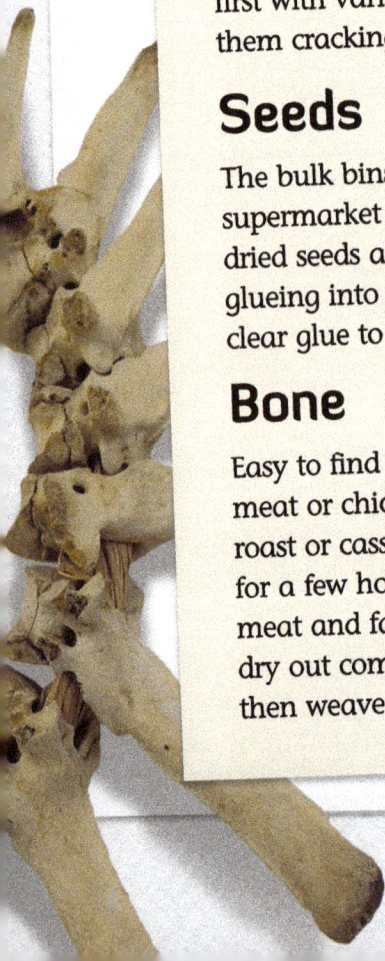

Pop(corn) Art

Painted popcorn, seeded with pearly beads.

This is a fun way of making texture. All you need is popcorn kernels and a saucepan or a popcorn maker. You can use readymade popcorn too but make sure it is unsalted, unbuttered and unflavoured.

Make your popcorn and let it cool down. (Eat some of it to keep your strength up!)

Use PVA glue to stick it onto paper, fabric or the surface you are wanting to decorate. Let it set (it might take a day) and then you can paint it. What does it look like to you? Coral, sea barnacles, fungus … or something else?

Harakeke (flax)

Flax is wonderful to weave. There are certain things to do when cutting harakeke in the Maori tradition. You must first give thanks to the plant (it's important to say thank you for anything!), then cut the leaves from the outside at the base of the plant. If you cut them from the middle, the plant will die. Always wash your hands before eating when working with flax, as the sap can give you an upset stomach!

You can work with the strips of flax as soon as you've cut them. Remember that whilst it looks lovely and green now, by the time you want to display your artwork it will have dried out and shrunk a bit. So think about how you want it to look when it's finished. If you want it to be green you might need to make your weaving from something else – fabric or plastic strips perhaps, or card painted green.

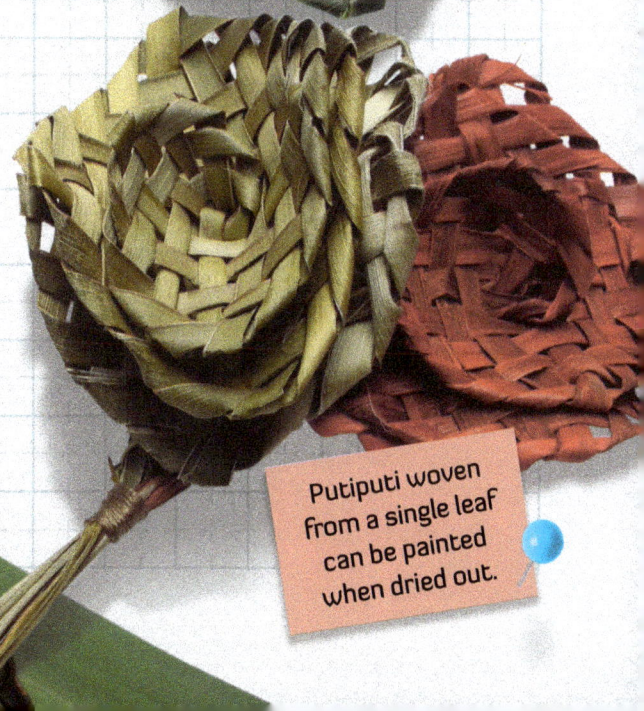

Putiputi woven from a single leaf can be painted when dried out.

51

ALL THAT GLITTERS

If you want something to really WOW the crowd, then anything that catches and reflects the light will really shine. But don't go overboard with it; remember what your concept is. If you are creating a serious piece of art about saving trees, for instance, then is glitter and shine something that will help tell your story? However, if it's about a magpie ... well then, start looking!

Rest the tin shape on a thick newspaper whilst you draw on the back of it. Turn it over and you will have a raised pattern.

Tin

Pie plates are a great source of lightweight tin. They are easy to cut with scissors and you can 'draw' patterns on them with a ballpoint pen.

Glitter

Yes, it is gorgeous ... but it makes a BIG glittery mess! If you must use it, glue it on with PVA glue and shake off the excess really well. It's a good idea then to seal it with a watered down coat of PVA. Keep a vacuum cleaner handy or you'll be finding glitter in your socks and hair for days!

Tin Foil

Tin foil is wonderful to scrunch up for lightweight shiny balls to hang off costumes. It's also good to glue down onto cardboard for shiny shapes. Use PVA glue.

1. Draw patterns onto card with hot glue then paint it with PVA.

2. Cover with tin foil whilst the glue is still tacky, and gently push it into the pattern.

CDs

Old CDs are perfect to hang off costumes, shiny side out. They are very hard to cut though, and when you do, the shiny coating peels off, so I suggest you use them whole or not at all.

Duraseal

This self-adhesive book covering material is not only useful for covering school books, but the foil ones, especially those with holographic patterns, are perfect for creating strips to 'bling' your art.

Mirrors

You can't use glass in your costume, but small acrylic mirrors from a craft shop are fine.

A glittery tassel made from a gum nut seed, sparkly wool and metallic gift wrap.

When you wish upon a star..

And how could anyone forget Christmas? Even if you don't celebrate it, you can use the decorations. The few days after Christmas are especially good for picking up very cheap decorations, and they will add glamour and sparkle to your costume. Stars, baubles, tinsel ... there to turn your creation into fantasy.

BUT WAIT, THERE'S MORE!

Here are some crazy things that people have used to make wearable art:

paint tin lids
socks
jigsaw pieces
curtains
kimonos
blankets
video tape
bottle tops
soft toys
dolls

venetian blind
car tyres
pens
umbrellas
pot plant holders
fly swats
dryer ducting
lightshades
baskets
tapa cloth

bamboo
zips
circuit boards
milk bottles
cutlery
kitchen strainers
jelly moulds
cake trays
umbrellas
human hair

yo-yos
egg shells
boxing gloves
mattress springs
used tea bags
knitting needles
wooden tea spoons
stuffed birds and hedgehogs!

The scales on this fish were made from fake fingernails!

What other odd things can you find?

CONSTRUCTION

How do I put it all together?

MEASURING

There is an old saying that builders use: **'Measure twice, cut once.'** If you have a carefully found and treasured piece of material, be it natural, manmade or recycled, you want to have it absolutely right *before you begin cutting*. Especially if you only have one of it.

Use a tape measure and a ruler. Write down every measurement and use a calculator if your maths isn't good. Your Wearable Wonder should fit your model, but it should also fit more than one person – just in case, on the day of the show, your model can't wear it because they got chicken pox, broke a leg or were just too shy to go out there on stage.

So make sure the garment is long enough and wide enough to fit a few different bodies. Allow a few centimetres overlap wherever it closes. You can always make a garment smaller but it's very difficult to make it bigger. If you are sewing seams on a machine, make sure you allow at least 1.5cm for the seams. This gives you room to let it out a bit if you need to.

Plan your garment and draw up a pattern.

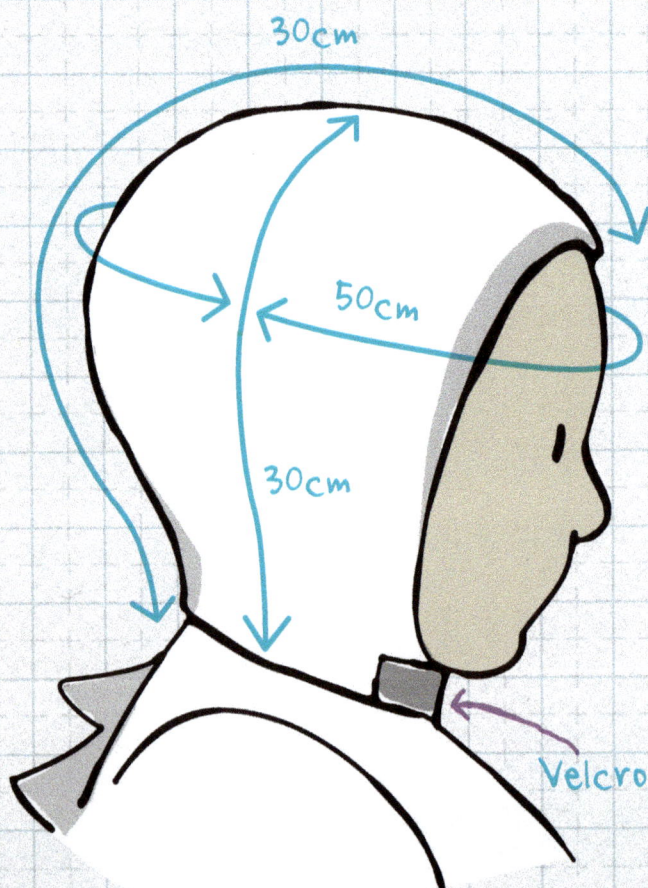

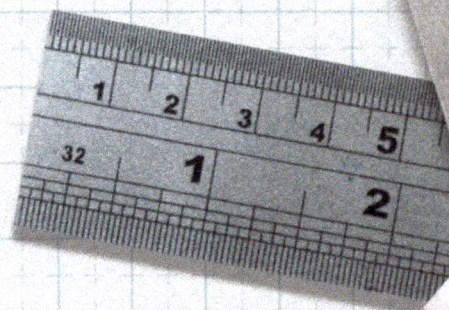

30cm

50cm

30cm

Velcro

PATTERN-MAKING

Did you make a small-scale model? It will give you a good idea of how many pieces are in the costume and if you need to make a special pattern for any of them. Make a paper pattern first before you cut any materials. Brown paper is really good for this. Draw on it with chalk. Dress patterns are useful for figuring out tricky things like sleeves; use them as a guide. Charity shops often have old patterns, so look for ones with the things you need – a skirt, a cape, a hood. They can all be changed and adapted, but they will give you a good understanding of how things fit together.

When you have drawn up your pattern pieces, cut them out and pin or tape them together on your model. You'll soon see where the garment does and doesn't fit.

Cut it out, you kids!

Pin or tape your pattern pieces to your fabric, card, paper, plastic or whatever material you are using. Trace around it with a pen or chalk and then start. Use fabric scissors, craft scissors or a craft knife, depending on what you are cutting. It's a very good idea to label your pieces 'front' and 'back', 'left' and 'right' with a bit of tape or a sticky note. It's amazing how often you can end up with two right wings, beautifully painted ...

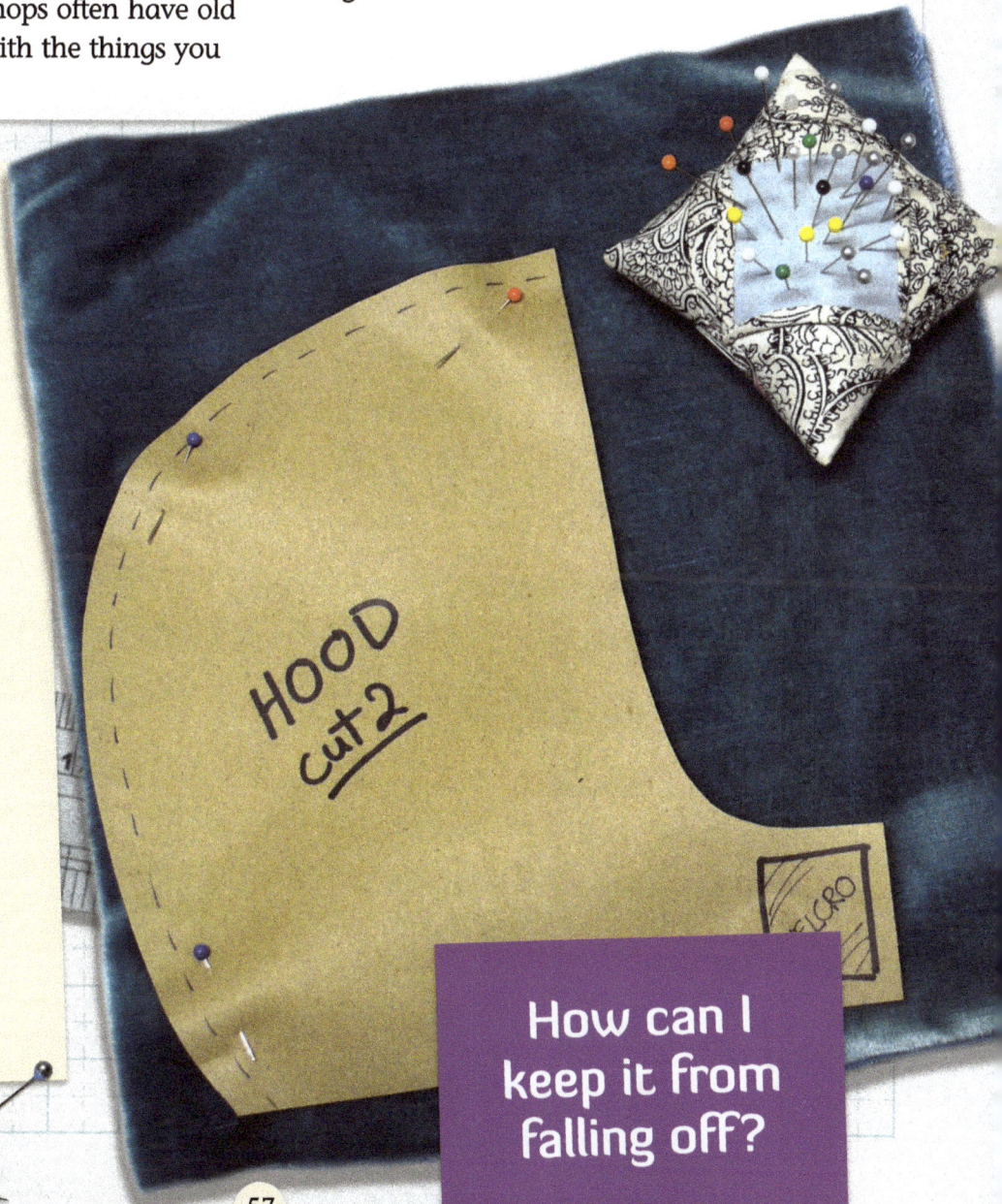

HOOD
cut 2

VELCRO

How can I keep it from falling off?

Sew easy

If you are using fabric, sewing is the best way of keeping it together. If you are working with cardboard and paper, you can use glue and tape.

Velcro and zips are the most traditional methods of keeping a costume done up. Zips are tricky to put in without lots of practice, but Velcro is easy. You can glue it in place with contact adhesive, but sew it on wherever you can, by hand or machine; it will be much stronger.

Make sure you use wide enough Velcro so that it can be adjusted to fit your model.

Elastic is another way of keeping your garment together but adjustable. Use wide black or white elastic from a craft or fabric shop to put in side, back and shoulder seams. Glue and sew into place.

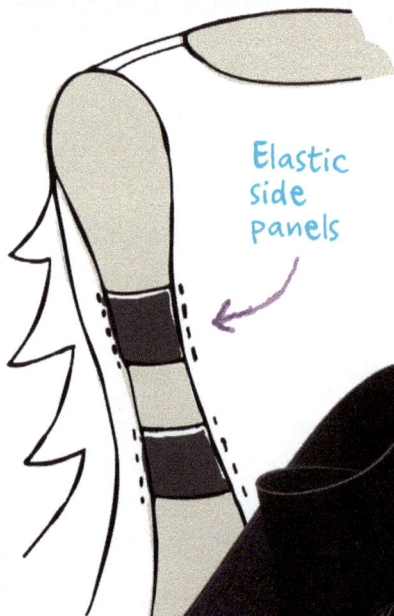

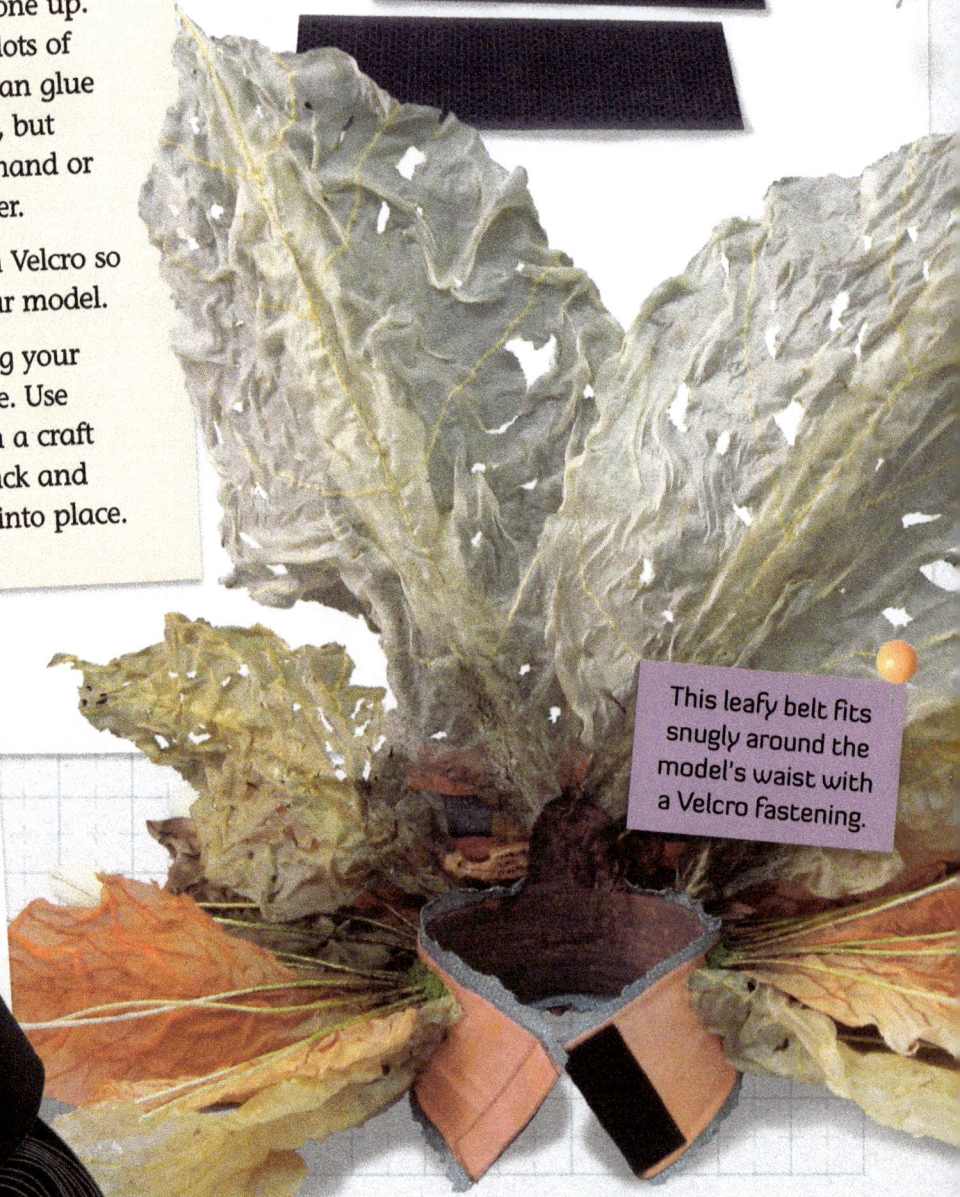

Velcro

Elastic side panels

This leafy belt fits snugly around the model's waist with a Velcro fastening.

Tie it

Cable ties are a really handy thing to have in your toolkit and can be bought at any hardware store or garden centre. They are great for joining plastic things together and, because they come in a variety of colours, you can match them to your costume. Once done up they are super strong and if you make a mistake, no worries – just snip them off with your scissors or side cutters.

You can also make cool accessories from cable ties.

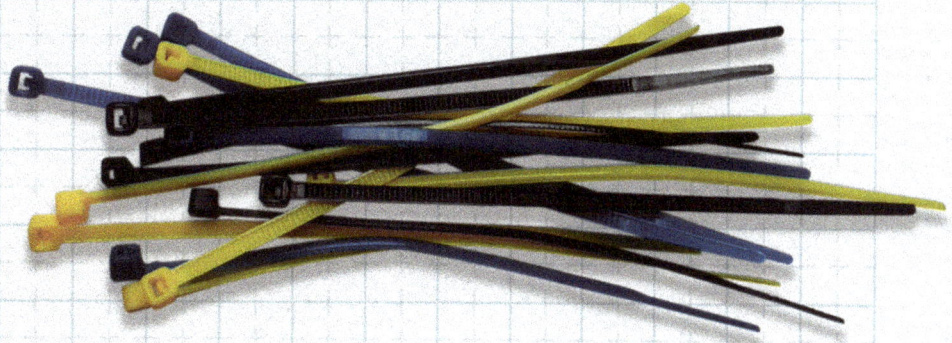

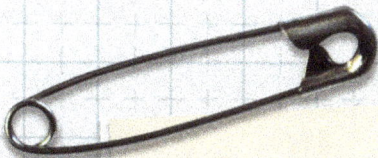

Pin it

Safety pins can be spray painted in all sorts of colours and used to hold stuff in place. A collection of safety pins in different sizes is a very handy thing to have in your toolkit.

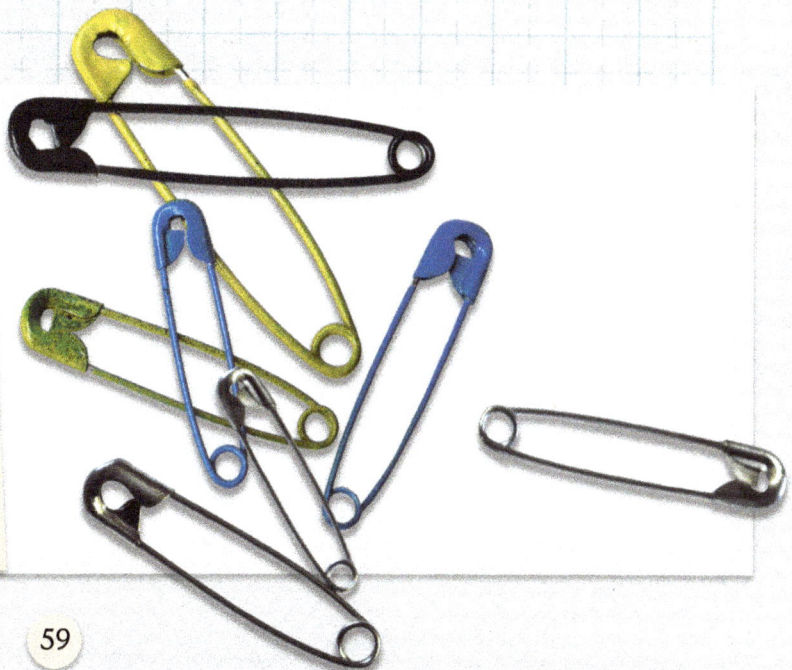

Wired up

Wire is very handy and comes in different thicknesses. Look for 'tie wire' or 'florist's wire' at a hardware store or garden centre. It's easy to bend and twist into shape. Great for creating shapes that you can build onto with foam and paper. Garden twist is excellent too; it's used for tying plants to stakes, but because it's covered in foam already, it makes a fantastic craft construction material. Wire netting is handy too, especially the plastic-coated stuff; better than chicken wire which can be pretty scratchy. Use your pliers and side cutters with wire – never use scissors unless you want to ruin them!

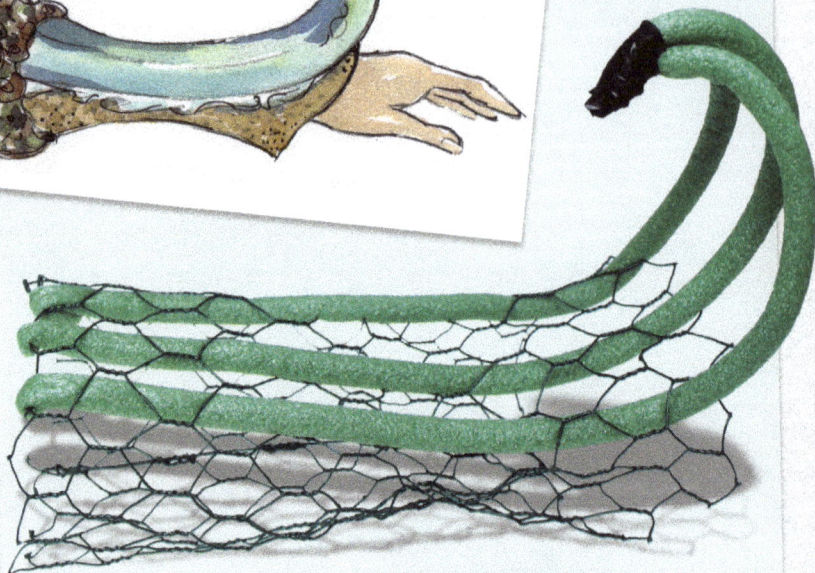

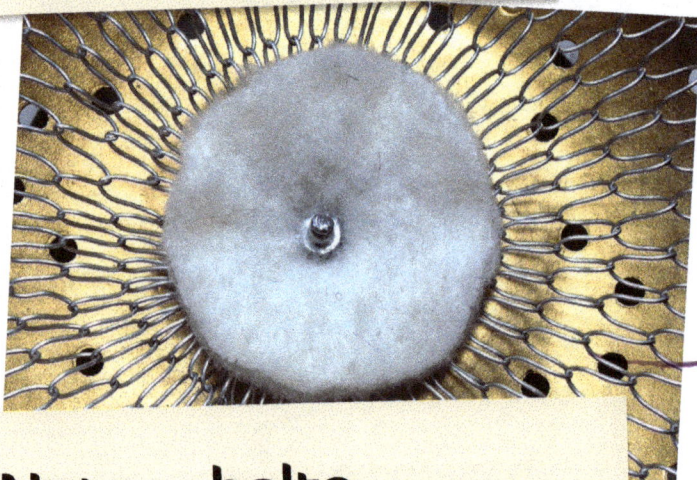

Nuts + bolts

Any part of your garment that will have stress on it and is in danger of pulling apart is best secured with hardware: good old-fashioned screws, nuts and bolts. Make sure that you snip the ends off with bolt cutters and cover with foam rubber, cardboard or leather so they don't dig into the model.

Some common kitchen items were used to make this hat.

DON'T FORGET YOUR HEAD!

...or feet,
or anything
in between

Hats and headdresses are great but only when they stay put. The best way to do this is to have a chin strap; use a hat base that comes with one already attached, such as an old bike helmet. You may have one at home that's a bit broken and no good for safety anymore; or perhaps it has Spongebob on it, which was cool when you were little but not now! Alternatively go to a charity shop and see if you can find one there.

Bike helmets are great fun to decorate – build onto them with recyclables and hot glue then spraypaint them for a spectacular result. They have the added advantage of built-in chinstraps to keep them securely on the head.

And it is hard to go past a pirate hat from a dollar-saver store. Take off the fabric and underneath is a perfect felt base just waiting for your creative touch. Easy to hot glue stuff onto or cover with papier-mâché.

Don't want to go over the top? Make a simple hat base from two strips of cardboard stapled together. Great for decorating with lightweight materials.

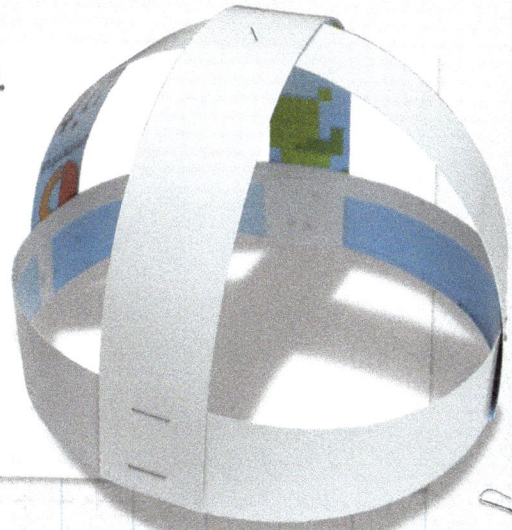

1 Bye-bye pirate ...

2 Hello, Papier-mâché ...

3 Add a plastic stalk, EVA foam curly bits and paint to make an acorn hat for a forest fairy.

If you make a costume that covers the whole head, make sure your model can see and breathe! A little netting painted the same colour as the outside of the costume will allow your model to do both.

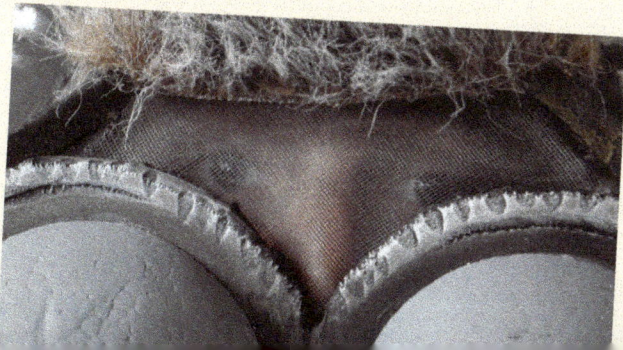

MASKS

A mask can change the whole look of your costume and is very useful when you might have to paint a face for multiple performances. Sometimes the simplest of garments with a very clever mask can be the most effective Wearable Wonder. You can spend a lot of time making a mask base, but the easiest way is to buy one from a craft shop or dollar-saver store and then build on top of that.

Avoid plastic mask bases; they are flimsy and hard to paint and decorate. The best ones are moulded from recycled paper, and they come in different shapes. You can paint them with acrylics and decorate them with anything you like, but they are also really wonderful to build onto with papier-mâché, cardboard and recyclables.

Try stretching fabric over the surface of the mask too. If the fabric is thin enough, the model will be able to see out of the mask without you cutting eyeholes.

Masks can be worn with the elastic band they come with, or you can attach a hood to them to cover the model's hair and neck. Make it a decorative part of your garment.

'Vena Immaculata' used a store-bought mask covered and draped with Lycra.

64

THE TAIL END

How can you make something that moves and adds to your garment? A tail can extend a costume, adding movement and interest. What creatures have tails? Dogs, cats, horses and cows, of course, but what else? Look at a lizard, monkey, bird, fish or lobster tail. What makes them interesting? Is it the scales, feathers, shape … or what the creature does with it? Does it bounce, drag, curl or slither?

Wire is good for making tails that curl and bounce.

Attach tails with a wide belt or sew them to the seat of your pants.

① Bend coated wire into the basic shape.

② Wrap it with wadding and cover it with fabric.

Cable tie sections together to make layered tails that move like an armadillo's behind.

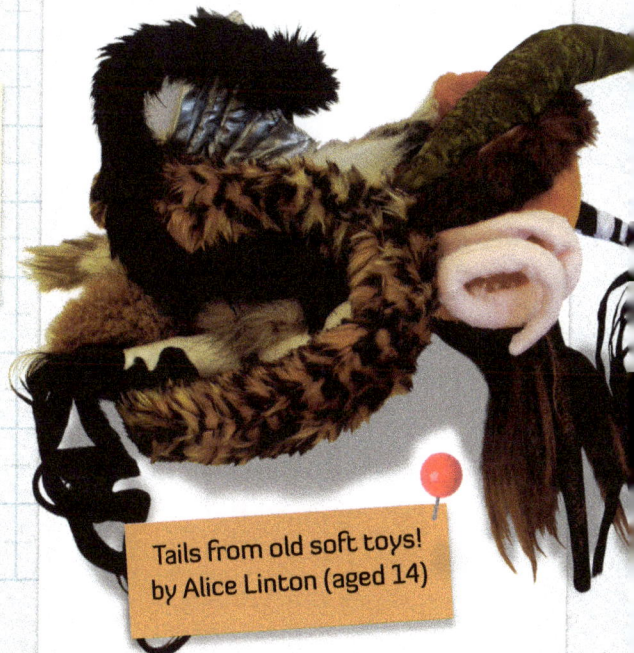

Tails from old soft toys! by Alice Linton (aged 14)

FLAPPING ABOUT

Wings make for wonderful movement on the stage, especially if you attach them to your arms.

A simple way to make wings is to use bamboo garden stakes. Sometimes you can get hooped ones, which make the process easier. Cover them in frost or shade cloth using double-sided tape.

If you want them to bend at the elbow, have the garden stakes start midway down the arm.

You may like to make frost cloth or paper feathers and glue or sew them on. Or for a dark and spooky theme, make holes in the shade cloth and give it raggedy edges. Perhaps you could add metallic paper strips to flutter and catch the light.

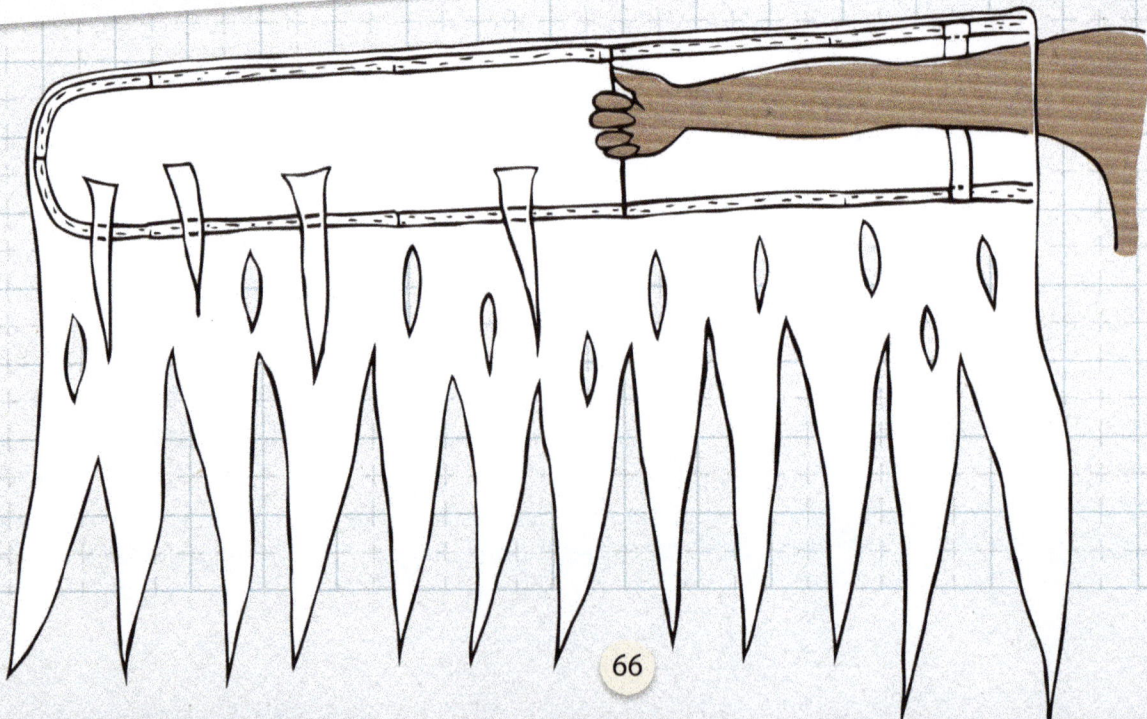

FINGERS TO TOES

If your costume allows for the model's legs, feet and fingers to show, then give them some thought. Are bare legs and arms good for your look or would your model be best wearing tights? Tights can make good arm coverings too – just cut a neck hole and pull them on.

Maybe you need longer arms?
Fly swats are useful for this. Wrap wadding around the handle and build hands/paws onto the flat part. Cover in fabric or hide under a cape.

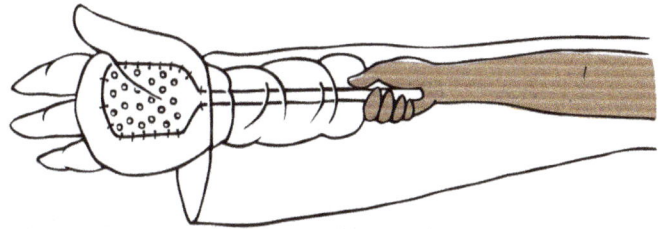

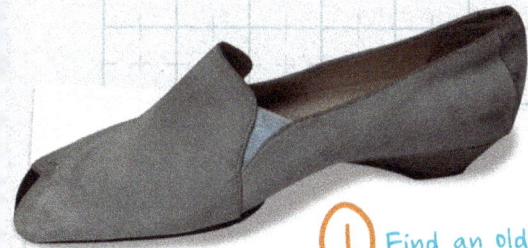

1 Find an old pair of shoes.

2 Glue anything onto them!

3 Paint and add finishing touches.

Would a really outstanding pair of feet complete your garment? You can build anything onto an old pair of shoes, from crocodile toes to robot boots.

By this stage, you will have put some of your garment together, but some of it might need to be painted first. It's often easier to do much of this before you finish construction, so let's take a look at paint and painting techniques to get the best look for your artwork.

A COLOURFUL STORY!

What should I paint it with?

BEST TYPES OF PAINT TO USE

Wherever you can, use water-based paint, e.g., acrylics. Oil-based paint needs turpentine to thin it and for cleaning your brushes. It's smelly and toxic to your skin and takes ages to dry. There's no real need to use oil-based paints when you can get great effects with acrylics. And if you want to make your work look shiny, finish it with a water-based varnish or watered down PVA.

Acrylic

Brushes wash clean with water but the paint dries waterproof. Acrylic is available in student colours (cheap), artist's colours (not cheap) and house paint (test pots are cheap). It's the best kind of paint to use for your creation. If you dilute it with water you can use it like watercolour paint. Get basic colours: black, white, red, yellow and blue. You can make all other colours by mixing them. And don't forget, all the colours mixed together will make brown.

Spray paint

Sometimes you need to cover plastic, tin or tricky surfaces to paint. Or maybe you want a really flat finish, or a metallic or fluoro look, or a clear glossy finish, then polyurethane sprays are the best thing to use. The only trouble with them is that they are really bad for your lungs, just like spray glue. So ...if you are going to use them, follow all the instructions on the can, use it outside in a sheltered area and wear a protective mask.

Always wear a mask when spray-painting, and do it outside!

① Create an up-cycled garment or accessory.

This collar was made from paper shred, bread bag ties, bottle tops, curtain hooks and artificial leaves glued together.

② Spray paint it.

The collar was spray painted with red and purple, then with white through a paper doily to create lace patterns.

Combing

Combing is great for creating wood grain effects and for creating patterns.

YOU WILL NEED:

- acrylic paint
- wide brush
- a piece of cardboard with notches cut out of it, or a thick comb

1. Paint a base colour first. If you are doing wood grain, make it a light yellow/brown. Let it dry.

2. Paint another colour on top and whilst it is still wet, drag the comb or cardboard through it.

   For wood grain, paint brown in patches and keep the lines uneven. You need to work quickly before it dries.

3. Try other layers of colour. Go from light to dark or dark to light. See what effects you can make.

Stipples and spatters

Stipples and spatters make effective stone textures.

YOU WILL NEED:

- Acrylic paint
- a thick paintbrush – a really scrubby, rough one!

Paint the base colour first. Let it dry.

Water down the paint and dip your brush into it. Flick it at the surface. For small areas, flick the bristles with your finger. An old toothbrush works well for fine splatters.

This technique is very messy, so make sure you put plenty of newspaper down first.

Dry Brushing

Dip the very tips of your brush in a lighter coloured paint. Don't water it down. Wipe off any blobby bits then dab and stroke the surface with the brush. Try layering lighter and lighter shades.

Sponging

Sponging is good for covering areas with texture and blending and creating patterns.

YOU WILL NEED:

- acrylic paint
- a sponge, or foam rubber offcut (pulling little bits out of your foam will make for great textures; cutting it into shapes will help you repeat patterns)

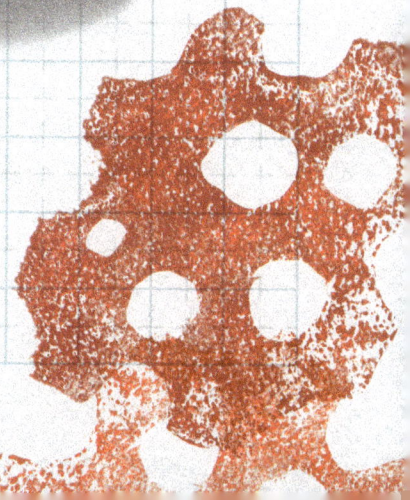

Paint the base colour first. Let it dry.

Dip your sponge into the paint and wipe off any excess. Dab it lightly onto the surface. Try layering different colours.

Antique metals

These are easier to create than you'd think. You don't need to buy expensive gilding materials when metallic paint is available.

YOU WILL NEED:

- black acrylic paint
- metallic paint (gold, silver or bronze)
- a paintbrush … and your fingers!

Glue buttons and beads to a base shape and paint the whole thing black.

Dip your finger into the metallic paint and rub it over the surface. (You can also do this using the 'dry brush' method if you don't want to end up with a shiny finger!) Let it dry between coats and build up the colour until it looks like metal. There is also an antiquing paste that comes in different metal colours that you can buy from art and craft stores. It's quite expensive but lasts for years. You only need a tiny little bit and it works really well. Finish off your 'antique metal' with clear varnish to give it a shiny finish.

Stencils

Stencils are perfect for making repeat patterns.

YOU WILL NEED:

- acrylic paint and thick brush, or spray paint
- tracing paper or thin card (manila folders are good for this)
- sharp craft knife
- a cutting mat

Trace the picture you want onto the paper or card. On a cutting mat, cut out the shapes with a craft knife.

Lay the stencil over the paper or object you want to decorate and dab colour over it with a sponge, brush or you can use spray paint. Lift the stencil off carefully and repeat.

So, you've designed it, constructed it and painted it, now what?

Give it a name, a short, cool, descriptive one, and then it's ...

SHOWTIME!

OMG!
OMG!
OMG!

It takes a group of people to turn a performance into a show.

Garment Designer

There might be more than one: someone to create a story (writer), someone good at construction (engineer), someone good at sewing (tailor) and someone good at painting (artist). Each has different skills to bring to the creation.

Model

Choosing a model is not about who is the prettiest. It's about who can make that garment move and tell the story: someone who isn't shy, who can wear the garment easily and will turn up on the day. And it's a good idea to have an understudy – someone who can stand in if the model gets sick. Remember that kids grow, so if you made the garment at the start of one term and it is being performed at the end of the next, your original model might not fit it anymore!

Wardrobe

Your model will need help to get into the costume: a couple of dressers to do up Velcro and zips, put on headgear, make sure wings are in the right place and that things float, fly, open and shut properly. They also help the model out of the costume and put everything back in its own box or bag. Label each piece of the garment so all the bits are kept together, and write a list to tape on the outside. A photos of how it should look is a good idea too.

The Wardrobe team must be able to make on-the-spot repairs, so a toolkit of scissors, safety pins, tape, glue and cable ties is essential.

Make-up and hair

It's good to have someone ready with hair ties, clips and hairspray, plus lipstick, face paints and brushes, and a box of tissues and face wipes.

Theatre Director

The job of the director is to decide when and where each Wearable Wonder fits into the overall performance and to make sure that all the teams work together to produce a wonderful show. The director is also the boss, so listen to him/her. If you have five directors, you'll end up with five different orders. So choose your director carefully; someone you respect and trust.

The wardrobe team must be able to make on-the-spot repairs ...

Music Director

Someone needs to be in charge of the music, not only to decide what kind of music will get played, but also to make sure it is on a device that is at the venue so it CAN be played. There is nothing more embarrassing than losing your soundtrack! Make sure that it works well with the story you are trying to tell. A dreamy, floaty soundtrack might work well for a story about flying but not for one about a tsunami.

Choreographer

A choreographer is a person who creates dance; working with the music to help your model show off the garment and all that it can do. Rather than dance, think 'movement'. Bending, swaying, twirling ... what shows the garment best? Exaggerate each move – make it big!

How will your Wearable Wonder enter the stage, perform, and then leave? Your model needs to know when to move on. If your stage has steps, make sure your model can get up and down safely in their costume.

Lighting and tech

Lighting can take the show from ordinary to extraordinary. Spotlights, disco balls, even handheld torches shining and flickering from backstage all help the with the WOW effect! How about a data screen with changing images in the background? You need a couple of technicians managing these things; making sure that there are enough power points, plug boxes, batteries, lights, cables and leads, and that they are all working on the day of the performance. And don't forget to bring a camera – you'll want a record of all your hard work!

Exaggerate each move – *make it big!*

'Kunugi Kodama' by Fifi Colston.

78

DRESS REHEARSAL

The team will have been working on their separate jobs up until now, but the dress rehearsal is when it all comes together: **lights, music, action!**

Make sure you leave enough time to have one. This will be where you will find out what does and doesn't work. You'll also find out if it's too long. You might need to make some last-minute changes and this is where you can make them. After the dress rehearsal, make sure all your garments are where they should be, your models aren't sick or away, your technical gear is working and you are all still speaking to each other. Then go and have some food and a rest because you can't perform well if you're tired and hungry.

So, all good?
Ready to WOW?

Then break a leg!

(An old theatre saying that means good luck ... yes, really!)

Backstage, World of Wearable Arts Award Show.

'Is it Socks?' by Alison Mackay and Gabrielle Edmonds, Lower Hutt.

INTERVIEW WITH A WOW MODEL

'Radiata Princess' by Petrina Yuretich, Ahipara

Sarah Ngan Kee

How many times have you been in the WOW show as a model and performer?

I have modelled three garments in the WOW show over four years from age 11 to 14. In my first year I was a performer in the Oceania Section. I was so excited to get through the auditions and be a part of it all! Hinewehi Mohi was singing in this section and we four models had to each bring in a piece of her 'dress', and attach it onto her. Coming onto the stage, I was lifted up and put onto the shoulders of two tall stage performers. It was definitely out of my comfort zone being up so high on an entrance, but I had a lot of trust in Paora and Jesse, who have performed in many previous WOW shows. For one show, they used a couple of us older kids in the UV section. It was difficult trying to dance in the dark but it was an awesome experience as it is one of my favourite sections of the WOW show. The cool thing was, we got to crawl under the stage in order to emerge at the right spot, and this introduced us to more of the background theatre kind of stuff.

What was the trickiest creation you wore?

The most difficult garment I wore was the year the children's section had a tutu theme. The garment I was wearing was completely made out of pine cones! (Radiata Princess, by Petrina Yuretich and Melanie Bradbury.) I felt a bit like royalty – the garment consisted of a crown of sliced pine cones behind my head and neck, a pine-needle body, and then the sliced pine cones tutu. It was quite heavy, stiff and poked into me a lot of the time. The WOW crew helped by lining the under-tutu part with a thin layer of foam and putting a layer of foam on my shoulders to make it more comfortable. Being stiff, this also made my movements a lot more limited, but Malia Johnston choreographed my dance in order to fit the garment, and what I could achieve in it. And once I got on stage, the pain disappeared! You get so lost in the performance that it is no longer an issue. I also really admired this garment, and felt so privileged to wear it.

What was the most fun one?

I feel my last garment 'I Feel Like A Princess Tonight' was the most enjoyable. Having had three years of experience of the WOW shows, I knew what to expect – commitment as well as stage presence. I felt more confident in performing the garment on stage as it was less restrictive. I also loved getting my makeup and hair done by a whole team of people. I would wait in line at the different stations (e.g. foundation, blusher, and eye makeup) for the team to fuss over me for their part, then pass me on to the next station.

How many times do you have to practice in the costume?

I wouldn't be able to give you an estimate of how many times we practised in them but most of the time on stage, we were in the costumes. We spent most of the rehearsal time in them to get used to them as the garments came in the strangest shapes and sizes! And since the garments are the reason for the show, it was important to make sure we make them look as well presented and represented as possible for the artists, thus, practising in them whenever we could.

How many times do you perform it during the whole WOW season?

We started off with two practices a week starting from August, but closer to the show it got to three times a week. Then every night for the show. It's hard to get sick of it though, being surrounded by such creative people, and closer to the time moving into the TSB venue made it even more exciting!

What advice would you give to a person making a garment?

Make the garments as comfortable as possible to wear. The models will stay happy and put on a good face with ease. Also make the garment sturdy. Sometimes they have to be fixed, glued, or sewn back together as they are so delicate. Try and make it as unrestrictive as possible to give the choreographer more to work with.

Have you one memorable story from your experience of modelling a particular garment?

When I wore 'I Feel Like A Princess Tonight', by Swati Gupta, it had actual lights in the castle top half of the garment, and a floaty cloud skirt. As the artist was from India, the garment was featured on national television over there, where she talked about it and explained her concept. It was great to be able to see the person who had made the garment I was wearing. I hadn't seen the artists in previous years, so it was a real privilege to be able to see this, and hear her views about the costume.

What made you want to model a WOW garment and would you do it again?

I love performing. And I just love the idea of WOW. I would definitely be a part of this experience again, mostly for the whole atmosphere of it all. Right from the back stage crew, to getting out in the spotlights performing to a huge audience, you are a part of a much bigger team and everyone has to do their bit and fit in to it all. WOW makes me feel proud to be a New Zealander as the whole thing was started by a Kiwi here in New Zealand, and it is growing in

Sarah Ngan Kee wearing 'I Feel Like a Princess Tonight' by Swati Gupta, India.

STAGE AND FILM

When I grow up...

(these people liked making stuff
when they were kids)

WOW®
WORLD OF WEARABLEART

weta workshop

When Dame Suzie Moncrieff was a girl, she loved dressing up for plays, and art. She and her family lived in Hope, Nelson with a house full of music and plenty of paper, pens, paints and dress-up boxes.

'When I was 8 I painted a picture of a Maori canoe in the sea and it was chosen by the Art and Craft Advisor to go on exhibition in Japan. This really encouraged me and helped me to believe I could be an artist.

After getting 93% in school certificate Art, Suzie sat Fine Arts prelim, just doing Art and English in her 6th form year. She passed in English but not in Art! "I was gutted, "she said. "I couldn't believe it. It seemed like my world fell apart and my future as an artist and attending Art School was never going to happen.

So Suzie went to Teachers' Training College and spent all her time in the art room making wire sculptures. Then she went out into the world and did all kinds of jobs including being New Zealand's first car saleswoman! But in 1985 Suzie started sculpting again and opened the William Higgins Gallery. However running a business and selling artists' work is hard work and no matter how hard you try, sometimes it just doesn't pay the rent. Suzie was feeling as if nothing was going right when she saw an exhibition in Auckland of art that was wearable, but it seemed to her that it was more about pretty dresses. This wasn't art as Suzie knew it, it was fashion.

"Being a sculptor, my mind ran riot with possibilities for a show featuring real art worn on the body in wildly wonderful ways. On that plane going home to Nelson, The World of WearableArt was born!"

A great show, the one that we are familiar with first in Nelson and now in Wellington with travelling mini shows and exhibitions around New Zealand and now internationally, doesn't just happen.

An old WOW team photo, with Suzie (front right) and Heather (front left).

Suzie spent hours knocking on doors, explaining her idea to people who didn't understand what she was trying to do. She asked for help, she asked for support and she didn't give up until someone 'got her'. That someone was Eelco Boswijk who was her first sponsor. So the first show took place, in her little gallery, and it was fun but shifting stage and props and cleaning up the portaloos afterwards was not very glamorous!

There was more work to come and some people might have just given up. But not Suzie. By 1990, she had convinced her sister

Heather Palmer to join her. It was a sell out show and they have never looked back.

"From day one it was a lot of fun, as well as hard work," says Heather, "but Suzie's passion to make the show successful meant I never really thought of it as work. It was a steep learning curve and I had to learn fast as I had no training in business finance but I had the passion and desire for the show and to achieve and learn something new.

"All these years later, I am still as passionate about WOW as I was at the very first show and look forward to the journey ahead."

> **As Suzie says:**
> "This was never about the money. If it was, it would have lasted five minutes."

WOW NOW

- Multi-million dollar business
- Employs 12 fulltime staff, and up to 400 at show time
- Attracts 60,000 visitors to Wellington
- Up to 400 hopeful NZ and international designers enter each year
- Around 100 garments selected for the show

Film, fashion, photography, craft, design, sculpting and drama are all called into play in Wearable Art. Experienced costume makers compete alongside novices to the art world – with surprising results. Many a nervous "I've never done art but like making things" first-time entrant has won a major prize. This show isn't about being a professional artist and earning a living from it. It's about following your passion and creativity.

Nelson, the birthplace of WOW, is still home for Suzie and Heather.

Suzie and Heather have their own pieces of wisdom for you when it comes to making and creating art and following your dreams.

So, what are you waiting for? The world is yours, put it on and make it wonderful!

> **Heather:** "Use your imagination and always have fun."

> **Suzie:** "Never give up!"

Weta Workshop sponsors a WOW show section with a prize that allows an aspiring costume designer to have 'work experience' in their Miramar workshop. They love to see new talent emerging via the show. WOW artists have worked on big films like *The Lion, The Witch and The Wardrobe, The Lord of The Rings* and *The Hobbit* because once, they thought, 'I wonder if I could make a ...'

When Sir Richard Taylor was a boy he loved making things. Whether it was sculpting, building papier-mâché monsters, making landscapes for his train set, hanging out with his dad in the small shed at the front of the house constructing things out of wood – or just sitting at his mum's sewing machine sewing up bits of clothing, Richard was always focused on creating things with his hands and loved the thrill of making things.

"When I was 10 years old I really wanted to build a big dragon for my bedroom. I blew up a balloon and stuck papier-mâché over it to build the initial body form. Then added cardboard tube legs and neck and other bits and pieces to create the head and the tail. I then painted it up with red poster paint and gave it great big round dots on its body. I was absolutely thrilled with this at the time and it sat next to my bed for many years."

Young Richard knew he wanted to make things with his hands and hoped that one day he would be able to do this for a job. He had no idea where his creative aspirations would take him but looked to a career in the creative arts.

At Wellington Polytech he studied visual communication and design. He quickly discovered that he was not a great illustrator or graphic designer and therefore set about trying to solve all of the teachers' briefs through 3-D sculpture and model-making.

Sir Richard Taylor and Tania Rodger.

Sir Richard Taylor with his model of Jane from Martin Baynton's *Jane and the Dragon*.

Fortunately the teachers saw his talent and Richard ultimately passed his three-year course having completed most of the projects in this way.

A business like Weta Workshop doesn't happen all by itself. A great team is needed, and Richard found his best teammate in Tania Rodger. Weta Workshop not only works in the areas of design, armour, weapons, creatures, miniatures, props and costumes, but they also do fine art sculptures, publish their own books, sculpt and manufacture high-end collectables for fans around the world, and enjoy making their own television and other creative projects within the workshop. Although Richard and Tania started their business in the back room of their flat, their company now sprawls throughout a large building in the Wellington suburb of Miramar and, on a big film such as *The Hobbit*, the crew may expand to 200 people.

ACKNOWLEDGMENTS

A book is a team effort and I would like to thank the following people in particular for their wonderful help and support whilst I created it. Firstly for my publishers for seeing my potential and suggesting I do this book; it has made me very happy. To Luke and Vida Kelly, our treasured book design team, who wrestled it into shape without throwing it at us.

And also to Rose Scheyvens and Cleve Shearer, enthusiastic leaders in education – our kids are in very safe hands with you; Ruth Hooke, school buddy from long ago and much loved drama and dance teacher who cast an experienced eye over 'Showtime'; Sarah Ngan Kee for her insightful interview; Nay Johnson whose generosity in lending me her superior camera knows no bounds; the lovely Beth Jones who modelled for me both on the stage for WOW and then again in my studio; Nautilus Creative Trust where I made things and found Jean Burgers' fabulous felt hats; Richard Taylor and Tania Rodger who were so willing to contribute their support, thoughts and inspirations to the book; Suzie Moncrieff, Heather Palmer and the team at WOW who embraced the book idea and who created this amazing event that I have so loved being a part of for the past 30 years and will continue to do so for as long as I can wield a pair of scissors!

And to my fellow WOW designers and Facebook community who 'liked' me and kept my energy up over one long hot summer whilst I sweated my way through creating images for this book. Knowing you wanted me to finish it kept me cool!

INDEX